FISH ON!

FISH ON!

A Guide to Playing and Landing Big Fish on a Fly

FLOYD FRANKE

THE DERRYDALE PRESS
LANHAM AND NEW YORK

THE DERRYDALE PRESS

Published in the United States of America
by The Derrydale Press
A Member of the Rowman & Littlefield Publishing Group
4501 Forbes Boulevard, Suite 200, Lanham, Maryland 20706

Distributed by NATIONAL BOOK NETWORK, INC.

First Derrydale Printing 2003
Copyright © 2003, Floyd Franke

Library of Congress Cataloging-in-Publication Data

Franke, Floyd
  Fish on! : a guide to playing and landing big fish on a fly / Floyd
Franke.
     p. cm.
Includes bibliographical references.
  ISBN 1-58667-070-0 (cloth : alk. paper)
  1. Fly fishing. I. Title.
  SH456 .F75 2003
  799.1'24—dc21

                                                          2002153419

♾™ The paper used in this publication meets the minimum requirements of
American National Standard for Information Sciences—Permanence of Paper
for Printed Library Materials, ANSI/NISO Z39.48-1992.
Manufactured in the United States of America.

Dedication

It is said that there are three stages in the life of a fisherman. The first, to find satisfaction in catching as many fish as he can. The second, to find pleasure in catching only the biggest fish. The third stage, to seek the challenge of only the most difficult fish. To these three I like to add still another, a fourth stage. This stage is reserved for those who find their satisfaction in sharing their knowledge for the benefit of those new to the sport. I dedicate this book to all who teach.

CONTENTS

CONTENTS

ACKNOWLEDGMENTS

No man is an island and no book has ever been written without the assistance of others. Many have contributed their time and talent to my endeavor. I am indebted to all and thankful for their help. There are a few individuals, however, who have gone far beyond the call of duty or what friendship would expect. I wish to acknowledge their special contribution for without them this book would not have been written.

To John McCollough, Ben Hunnicutt Jr., and Robert Triggs. Their candid comments and thoughtful suggestions as "readers" were most helpful.

To Gordon "Gordy" Hill, saltwater fly fisher extraordinaire, who shared his knowledge freely to make this book more saltwater friendly.

To Joan Wulff for her unwavering support and encouragement.

To Kermit Hummel who first suggested that I write the book and who stayed by my side, first as my editor then my friend. He has been a constant and guiding light.

Finally, to my wife, Alberta, who for over forty years has stood at my side to offer her unconditional support and encouragement for projects past, present, and future. No man has ever had a more devoted and loving wife.

FOREWORD

Joan Salvato Wulff

This is a unique book in that the majority of angling literature focuses only on techniques for getting the quarry to *take* the fly. While most anglers agree that the strike *is* the ultimate high—the moment of truth—there is the further goal of today's anglers to land the fish as quickly as possible in order to return it to the water unharmed. This book will help you to do just that by expanding your horizons far beyond the long-standing, perfunctory rules: "rod tip up," "keep pressure on," and "don't give 'em slack!" Rules by rote are limiting—a real handicap to the thinking angler who delights in the challenges a hooked game fish can provide.

Floyd Franke gained his first understanding of how and when to break these rules as an instructor at the Wulff School of Fly Fishing, under the guidance of Lee. Lee, a fisherman and outdoor filmmaker, had developed his skills to the point of making hooked fish "act" for the camera.

Once Floyd had experienced success in giving rainbow, brown, and brook trout slack line on purpose, *he* was hooked too, and playing large fish became a mission. His skills expanded as he experienced catching wild steelhead, salmon, and the myriad saltwater species, noting how their very different environments and personalities could affect playing strategies.

Today's angler is mobile, with fishing opportunities of greater variety than ever before: you may be trout fishing this week, perhaps hunting tarpon next week. Knowing the fighting characteristics and escape strategies of the various species and how to counteract them will add to your success ratio.

A gifted teacher, Floyd also shares with the reader the importance of decisions made long before the fishing trip begins, such as choosing tackle components that will facilitate both the presentation and the playing challenges. He explains the dual role of rod actions; reel design, capacity and braking systems; and choices of knots for the various connections—ones that won't come undone under pressure.

For inexperienced anglers, landing a big fish is usually pure luck. *Controlling* a hooked fish is a learned skill. These pages are packed with strategies and techniques for use in this regard: the relative position of the angler and hooked fish for applying pressure (on foot or in a boat), how to keep the fish from running out of the pool or into trouble, walking a fish upstream, knowing the true strength of your leader tippet and when and how to use it, and something previously unexplored: the psychology of breaking a fish's will!

It's all here. Outstanding coverage of a complex and challenging subject!

Playing fish skillfully is an extension of the catch and release ethic. With the intention of returning the fish to the water unharmed, an angler's landing and releasing techniques are yet another important element. And, when things go awry and there is no fish to release, Floyd gives you the tools to analyze *why*!

The standards by which to judge yourself in this exciting endeavor are in your hands. Practice these techniques and take extra pride in landing the biggest fish of your life, knowing it wasn't just a matter of luck!

INTRODUCTION

Why is it that as fishermen we spend hundreds of dollars on equipment and invest hours of our time working to improve our fish-catching skills and yet spend so little time working to improve our fish-playing skills? As I reflect on my own fishing experiences, I can see the same casual inattention to playing fish as I often see in others. Even the sportswriters have given it little attention. Certainly it is possible to find an occasional article that offers a tip or two about playing fish under special circumstances, but never a comprehensive work designed to acquaint the reader with the underlying theory and practice of playing fish. Why is it that this aspect of our sport has been given such low priority, when reason would seem to dictate otherwise?

Looking back into my fishing past for an answer to this riddle, I see that when I was just beginning to fish in the early 1950s, my first concern focused on being able to get my bait out far enough to where the fish were feeding.

Lobbing and later true casting techniques were developed to accommodate the changes in equipment, which began with a twelve-foot cane pole, followed by a bait casting rod and reel, and reached its zenith with a super effective, high-tech spinning outfit purchased in 1961. As I became more competent in my ability to place my bait where I wanted it, my attention began to shift more and more toward being able to catch fish under all conditions. I fished every chance I got, read magazine articles and books on the subject, and listened to and watched those whose skills exceeded my own. And so I learned how to catch fish in the spring when the water was high and later in the heat of the summer when the water levels dropped and temperatures rose. Still, there were times when the fish would pay little attention to my offering of live bait and so I undertook the challenge and learned to fly fish. Nowhere in the recollections of my first thirty years of fishing can I recall having given serious attention to learning to play fish. I fought and successfully landed many fish, hundreds I am sure, and lost many others. Sometimes the hook would pull free, but most often the line or leader would break. But somehow, in spite of all the losses, I never felt compelled to improve my skills. How strange.

So, probing still deeper into my past experiences, I can now see that I was under the general impression that there was little more to playing fish than keeping the rod tip up, keeping the pressure on, and never allowing slack in the line. For me these three simple rules learned over a span of several years summarized all that I needed to know about playing fish. I was convinced that if I did all these things I would land the fish. That is, of course, providing that the fish was not too big for the line or leader I was using, in which case there was little if anything that could be done about it anyway. The often-heard lament that "The fish was so big he broke me off" gives expression to this common belief, which even today acts as a governor to keep our imagination in check. Those of us who were fishing in the 1950s, 1960s, and 1970s chose tackle that would be considered too heavy by today's standards. We were, in addition, careful to keep our rod tip up, the pressure on, and never to allow any slack in our lines. We landed enough fish to keep us satisfied and were delighted when Lady Luck smiled and a bigger than average fish was brought to the net. We were doing the best that could be expected and felt little need to change the way we were playing fish. However, things were beginning to change.

The earliest change began to take place in the late 1960s with the development of Michigan's steelhead program. These mighty anadromous rainbows caught the eye of thousands of fishermen who soon learned that hooking these leader-shy fish was difficult, especially when the sun was on the water. Anglers using lighter than usual lines, four- rather than eight-pound test line, scored well above the average on the number of hookups, but also led the field in the number of fish lost. Four or five fish were broken off for every one landed.

It was about this time that Dick Swan, from Clare, Michigan, and Ellis McColly from Midland, began experimenting with rods made from solid fiberglass "bike" sticks that children used on their bikes to make them easier to see in traffic. Selected because of their extreme suppleness, these bike sticks were transformed into long, limber rods designed to act as a super efficient shock absorber capable of protecting the finest lines from the stress of battle, which under normal conditions, using the stiffer rods of the day, would not have survived the first violent run of a hooked fish. And so the "noodle" rod and shortly thereafter a method of fishing called "light lining" or "ultralight fishing" was created.

The noodle rod attracted a great deal of attention because it allowed the use of extremely fine two-pound test line to land fish weighing four, five, even six times that much. Its appeal, however, was limited since the required suppleness of the rod renders it unsuitable in fly rod design and for powerful rods built for heavy use where stealth was of little concern. But, when all was said and done, we realize that the notion about big fish always getting away was not written in stone and with ingenuity they too could be landed. The psychological barrier that kept us from challenging how and why we played fish the way we did had finally been broken. Nevertheless, there was little change in fishing practices. Change it seems had to wait until the demands for greater stealth, expanded fishing opportunities, and increased interest in the practice of catch and release were obtained. The process took almost twenty years.

There is little doubt that fish respond to recurring threats in their environment by making changes in their daily habits. Their very survival is keyed to being able to fulfill their basic requirements for safety, food, comfort, and procreation. Increased fishing pressure alters how and when fish feed. They abandon their more casual feeding behaviors in favor of a more cautious approach. I have seen brown trout on the more heavily fished sections of the Beaverkill in upstate New York follow a fly for as long as twelve feet only to reject it, leaving the fly, but not the angler, undisturbed. Freshly stocked hatchery fish, on the other hand, make easy targets for fishermen. Raised in protected rearing pools, these fish judge all food as being safe. They grow gluttonous and eat without fear or the need for caution. Many of these fish will die; only the number of times that they will be caught before doing so is in question. If stocked in a controlled catch and release area and handled carefully when being released, a fish may be hooked a dozen or more times, sometimes several times in a single day. Only those fish that can adapt quickly to their new environment and learn from their mistakes have a chance at survival. They must learn caution and be quick to spot fraud. Any evidence of a dragging fly or glint of light off a heavy tippet must send them dashing for safety. As the fishing season progresses, only the most fit will survive to join the ranks of holdover fish from other stockings as well as wild stream bred counterparts. They now become difficult to catch and are thus worthy of our highest regard. They are a challenge to our skill and tackle.

The difficult task of outwitting these paradigms of cunning has led most of us to use lighter and lighter tippets, following an earlier path, sans the noodle rod, blazed by Dick Swan and other Michigan steelheaders. However, the use of lighter lines increased the likelihood that a fish would break off. In an effort to improve their hook-up/break-off ratio, some fishermen, both old and new alike, have turned to technology hoping to gain some advantage by using the new fluorocarbon lines and leaders. Stealthy but overly stiff by comparison with monofilament materials, their use is of marginal benefit and, because they are nonbiodegradable, may also pose a threat to wildlife. Technology is a false prophet, for its advantages pale when compared with those offered through improvement of one's fish-playing skills. Nevertheless, the growing use of fluorocarbon lines and leaders is a reliable indicator of the need for greater stealth as perceived by anglers today.

As a guide on the Beaverkill I have watched fishing-related fads come and go over the past fifteen years. I can remember the year when just about everyone had a wading staff hung from their vest. Next was the red handkerchief tied around the neck. That fad was followed by the wearing of wide-brimmed hats; followed by the SUV invasion. It seems that every year or so a new fad is born. Most last a year or two then pass into oblivion. But one fad that emerged near the end of the millennium and seems to have real staying power is the desire to travel to far-off fishing destinations. Quite a contrast from times past when a "local expert" was just that, a person who fished local waters for years and never went much beyond the next county.

Today's traveling anglers seek out locations and target species that boggle the mind. Peacock bass in Venezuela and Nile perch in Egypt. It is not uncommon to have students in my beginning casting classes tell of their experiences fishing for brown trout in Chile or Atlantic salmon in Norway. Their rush to broaden their fishing experiences is often matched by the rush to learn as quickly as possible fishing skills comprehensive enough to cover the wide variety of species and fishing destinations available. Frontiers, a leader in international fly fishing travel, includes twenty countries in their list of travel destinations and targets every fish species from albacore to wahoo. Is it any wonder that fishing "how to" books have become so popular? So much to learn and so little time to learn it. High on the angler's list of things to learn is an approach to fighting fish that is comprehensive enough to meet the challenge of such a wide variety of fish and fishing situations. However, as compelling as the need for this information may be, the need to play fish in a manner that does not kill them in the process is of special importance in our time.

By far the greatest change affecting our present need to know more about playing and landing fish occurred with the adoption of the catch and release ethic fathered by Lee Wulff. Catch and release is built on the belief that a game fish is just too valuable to be caught only once. Each fish caught and released lives to fight again, and in this way it is one angler's gift to another. However, to reach its full potential, each released fish must be returned in good condition. Played to exhaustion, most fish will die within twelve hours after their release. Although resuscitation before release can reduce mortality, fish-playing strategies designed to bring a fish quickly to net without undue physical harm should be a foremost consideration for today's conservation-minded anglers, and this will be discussed at length in chapter 7. And so, while there is little doubt as to the growing need for a comprehensive investigation of how we play fish, some confusion will undoubtedly arise as to how one goes about defining what is a big fish.

Those who fish for a place in the record book are far more critical in their judgment than most fishermen who would be satisfied to call "big" any fish that is larger than the average fish being caught at any location on any given day. But from the perspective of playing fish, I consider as big any fish that is capable of easily breaking my line unless reasonable care is given to how it is played. Hence, it is the relationship between the size and fighting ability of the fish and the strength of the equipment being used that will determine for me what is a big fish. Any fisherman who, for example, can land a twenty-five-inch trout weighing five pounds on 7X tippet in fast water can be proud of his accomplishment and rightly claim to having caught a big fish. By the same reasoning, a hundred-pound sailfish landed on ten-pound test line would also be considered a big fish.

While the need for increased understanding and skill in playing big fish arises from the changing nature of our sport, its true significance lies in the sense of accomplishment and awe that follows anytime an angler lands a big fish. These are feelings so powerful that at times they cause us to forget trouble, sickness, and hardship and to rejuvenate our souls. What benefits the soul is worthy of our special attention in both the preparation and in the doing. Now is the time for a comprehensive investigation of how to play big fish.

In addition to the general rules and techniques for playing fish, this investigation will look at those variables, often overlooked, that have a direct impact on our ability to play fish. These variables include our choice of equipment, the conditions under which we fish, and the particular species of fish we hope to catch. This comprehensive view is unique to fishing literature and is my contribution to it. The information comes from a variety of sources—from books, lectures, stores, conversations, and my own personal experiences. Of particular importance to the writing of this book has been my affiliation with Joan and Lee Wulff.

I joined the staff of the Joan and Lee Wulff School of Fly Fishing as an instructor in the spring of 1989. Time spent with Lee from then until his death in April 1991 provided a wealth of information. I have drawn heavily upon Lee's knowledge in the writing of this book, especially with regard to chapters 1 and 2. For those who may not be familiar with Lee Wulff, let me say that he was one of a very few men of his time to devote his life to fishing. His early education as an artist and later his self-taught skills as photographer, filmmaker, and author, even his love for flying, in one way or another involved fishing. In addition to his many talents, Lee was a thinker. He had a curious nature and acute powers of observation. This combination gave us the fishing vest, salmon tailer, the unique Wulff fly patterns, and many theories of fishing that serve to make us all more successful as fishermen.

After Lee's death, I was assigned to teach his lesson on "How to Play Fish" to our students at the Wulff School. As I became more comfortable with this assignment and as my interest in playing fish grew, Joan Wulff encouraged me to develop the lesson into a program that I could take on the road. I did my first program at a fly fishing show in the winter of 1994. The audience's response to this and the many programs since convinced me that within the world of fly fishing there was both an interest and a need for more information on the subject.

Although this book is directed toward those who fish with a fly rod, spin fishermen and plug casters will find the same basic fish-playing principles apply. Any who are willing to make the substitutions to the text that are required to bridge the problems generated by the differences in equipment used will find the book equally informative. What might appear in this book as a bias in favor of the freshwater angling is a reflection of my own development. My interest in fighting big fish began with trout and salmon and then expanded to include most of our popular saltwater species. This is the same path traveled by many of today's great saltwater anglers. There is a common core of knowledge that is shared by both groups. Where serious differences between freshwater and saltwater practice exists, I have noted them.

To those who target really big, offshore species such as bluefin tuna and blue marlin, I apologize. You will find little of value on the subject. This book will find its audience among those who target freshwater and inshore game fish. It is for them that the book was written.

ONE

THREE RULES FOR
PLAYING BIG FISH

Knowing the three basic rules of playing big fish is at the heart of playing fish in general. It is the simplest form possible and has served as the starting point for almost every fisherman, past, present, and, in all likelihood, will continue doing so far into the future as well. To keep the rod tip up, to keep the pressure on, and to not allow slack is about as uncomplicated as it gets. But the three rules are only a starting point. Learning the rules is followed by learning when to break them.

Chances are that if you were to meet my good friend and fishing partner Roy Ohman, he would tell you about the first time we fished together. Roy had invited me over to fish with him near his home on the Delaware River. By the time I arrived in the evening the hatch was just about to begin and the weather was perfect. The evening showed great promise as Roy and

I headed to the river. It didn't take long for Roy to get into a fish, a rainbow of about fourteen inches. I heard him mutter something like "oops it's gone." The battle was over almost before it had begun. We both returned to our fishing when again it was Roy who disturbed the quiet with a hoot. I turned to see that he was into another fish. I stopped fishing to watch as the fish streaked away downstream. Much to my surprise, Roy gave little line and I watched as the tension on both rod and line increased until the tippet broke. I offered some words of condolence then went back to my fishing. When the situation repeated itself just a short time later and Roy lost his third fish, I felt compelled to offer some advice. "Roy," I said, "you sure do keep those fish on a tight rein. Perhaps it would help if you took the pressure off and let them make that first run." He chuckled and thanked me for the advice. I breathed a sigh of relief that he was not offended by my intrusion into his fishing and went back to my own. Wanting to get into the action myself and being unfamiliar with the river, I asked Roy for help choosing a fly pattern to try. He gave me a fly, which I was quick to tie onto my 6X tippet. The fly worked its magic and I was into a fish on my second drift. Just as I was about to release I heard Roy hoot a fourth time. Another fish was heading down river, but this time he did not try to stop it as before. Almost as quick as he had made the strike, he broke with his practice of always keeping the pressure on and lowered the rod tip and let the fish take line. At the end of the run the fish was still on and was landed shortly thereafter. Roy went on to catch and land another fish that night and I did the same. To this day he still reminds me of that first time together. "You sure do keep a tight rein on those fish" he will say and chuckle good-naturedly. I think that Roy would agree that knowing the rules and when to break them is a good starting point for learning how to play big fish.

Keep the Tip Up

The scene is set anytime an angler hooks a fish in the company of others. You can bet money on the fact that sooner or later someone is going to shout "Keep the tip up!" Keeping the tip up gives expression to the importance of the rod as a fish fighting tool. More specifically, the rod serves as a shock absorber and by keeping the tip up you maximize this function. Be careful, however, not to raise the tip too high.

Maximum function as a shock absorber is achieved when the handle of the rod is held at a right angle to the fish you are playing. (See figure 1.1.) A rod held at an angle of considerably less than ninety degrees, let's say forty-five degrees, offers power to pull, but functions poorly as a shock absorber. Increasing the angle of the rod beyond the optimum ninety degrees, let's say to 135 degrees, will also cause the rod to function poorly as a shock absorber. It should be noted that as the angle is increased beyond ninety degrees, there is an increased risk of breaking the rod due to overstressing the more delicate tip section. Although a rod held high above the head as in the Orvis logo has some advantage in clearing line on the water, it offers no improvement in terms of shock absorbency over a rod held at the same angle but at waist level.

During the heat of the battle as the fish turns suddenly, accelerates, jumps, or dives, the rod tip is often pulled down toward the water. Mindful of the need to have the rod function as a shock absorber, our angler concentrates on keeping the tip up. Should he fail to do so a chorus of "Keep your tip up" will be there to direct him.

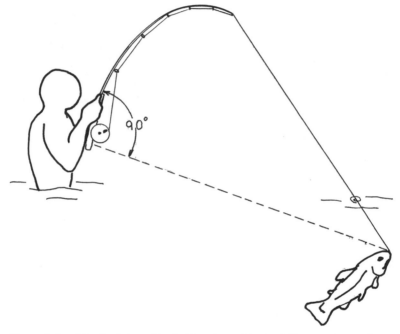

Figure 1.1. The Rod As a Shock Absorber—Vertical. The maximum function of the rod as a shock absorber is acheived when the handle and short section of the rod shaft adjacent to it are held at a right angle (90 degrees) to the fish you are playing.

But, is this really the best thing to do? What happens to the fish when you raise the rod tip?

As the rod tip is raised, the increasing angle of the tight line forces the fish to rise toward the surface. Since the last place the fish wants to go is up, except in an attempt to throw the hook, the fish struggles all the harder to gain depth. A fish out of control and thrashing wildly is even more likely to escape than a calm fish being heavily pressured. So what to do? Lower the rod angle in an attempt to help calm the fish, or raise the rod to gain maximum shock absorbency? Fortunately, this choice is an unnecessary one since the optimum ninety-degree rod butt-to-fish angle can be used to provide maximum shock protection regardless of which plane the rod is in. (See figure 1.2.) Although figures 1.1 and 1.2 show only two rod planes, vertical and horizontal, your options are not that limited. The rod can be held in any plane, including being inverted and held upside down. With the rod tip near the water and the rod handle held waist high, pressure is brought to bear on the fish at a very low angle. It is important that you understand that the rod can function as a shock absorber in any plane, and it does this job best when the ninety-degree butt-to-fish angle is maintained. With the requirements for maximum shock absorbency met, the angler is now free to attend to controlling the fish, using the position of the rod to direct applied pressure to maximum benefit. How does rod position affect our ability to control or play a fish?

Raising the tip of the rod when the line is tight may cause the fish to rise or be brought to the surface. This can be good if the fish is tired and you need to bring it to the surface and into your waiting net, but bad if the fish is fresh and responds violently.

When the tip of the rod is held low and to the side, the applied pressure serves to pull the fish's head to

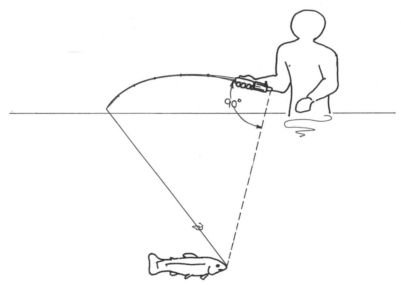

Figure 1.2. The Rod As a Shock Absorber—Horizontal. The maximum function of the rod as a shock absorber is achieved when the handle and short section of the rod shaft adjacent to it are held at a right angle (ninety degrees) to the fish you are playing.

one side, causing it to alter its course. In more extreme cases, this may cause the fish to be thrown off balance or to become momentarily disoriented. The fish responds by working hard to keep its head facing forward and its body upright. Not only is this hard work and very tiring, it forces the fish to abandon its other more aggressive escape responses such as running or diving. Playing a fish with the rod tip held low and to the side also allows the angler to steer a fish away from obstacles.

Steering requires overcoming the straight line momentum generated by the fish as it propels itself forward. This is not easy to do with the rod tip held high. When the rod tip is held low and to the side, however, the fish begins to lose momentum as its balance becomes threatened. Its straight line course becomes a curving one, and its ability to fight diminishes. Thus compromised, the fish loses some of its ability to determine where it is going and the fisherman gains the ability to more directly steer it. When not used to avoid obstacles, the technique of steering a fish can be used to keep the fish off balance and disoriented. In this case the angler applies pressure first from one side to the other, changing whenever the fish appears to have gotten its equilibrium back from the last maneuver. Some anglers overuse this side-to-side rod technique by changing positions too quickly, before the fish has had a chance to make its countermove. The only one in danger of becoming disoriented is the angler himself.

Keeping the tip low and to the side when playing a fish offers many more advantages than the more common practice of keeping the rod tip high. However, it would be foolhardy to abandon the tip high option altogether since there are situations that require it.

One situation that requires keeping the rod tip high is when you are trying to avoid obstructions on the surface of the water such as reeds, rocks, and mangrove shoots. Another closely related situation would be if you needed to remove a lot of slack line from the surface of the water in an effort to reduce the unwanted drag it creates. Picture a bonefish making a long, arching run through a forest of mangrove shoots or a salmon running through a field of boulders and almost instinctively your arms will begin to rise. Trust your instincts in this situation for that is just what you need to do. Keeping the rod tip high to avoid obstructions is common to both fresh- and saltwater fishermen.

Keep the Pressure On

This second rule is grounded in the belief that to keep the fish pulling against a tight line will tire it. While this is true in a general sense, constant pressure throughout the battle will spell disaster. Pressure must be applied smoothly from light to heavy in accordance with the dictates of circumstances that present themselves in the course of the battle. What the fish is doing, the location of the fish to the angler, and even how long the battle has been going will all have an impact upon the amount of pressure that can safely be applied.

If the movements of either fish or fisherman creates a situation where no line is coming in or going out through the rod guides, the condition is said to be static. If, on the other hand, line is coming in or going out through the rod guides, the condition is said to be dynamic.

Static conditions exist when, for example, a fish sulks, taking a position and refusing to move, or when both fish and fisherman are moving at the same speed and in the same direction, as can occur when fishing from a boat. It is under static conditions that the angler can safely apply maximum pressure.

Lee Wulff would demonstrate the concept of static conditions and maximum pressure to students of the Wulff Fly Fishing School by tying the tippet of his fully rigged six weight fishing rod to the porch of the classroom building. He would pass the rod to a student, inviting him or her to exert as much pressure as he or she could without breaking the tippet. Slowly the student would apply pressure then stop. Lee would encourage the student to continue. The bend of the rod would deepen. Fearful that the line or rod would break at any moment, the student would stop once more. Again, the student would be urged to continue. Straining to apply the pressure and beginning to show signs of tiring, Lee would ask the student whether or not he had ever before put that much pressure on a fish. "No" was the answer expected and received. Lee would then encourage the student to apply even greater pressure until finally the tippet broke. "How heavy was the tippet?" Lee would ask. Answers ranging from ten to twenty pounds were most common. Imagine the student's surprise when it was revealed that the 5X tippet had a breaking strength of less than five pounds.

Lee's porch pulling demonstration, as we refer to it today, reveals that without proper instruction, the average fisherman will never realize the full potential of his equipment and thus fail to use it to its full advantage. I do not have to look very far back into my developmental years as a fisherman to realize how often I had misjudged my tackle. Often I would blame it for not meeting my expectations, only to discover later that through my misuse of it, I was to blame. Maximum pressure can safely be applied to a fish you are playing only when conditions are static.

Any movement of the fish or angler can bring about dynamic conditions that will dictate changes in the amount of pressure applied. Not releasing pressure when a fish runs is not only the most common fault of the beginner but one that plagues seasoned anglers when confronted with a new and faster quarry than that to which they are accustomed. Let my personal experience with false albacore after a steady diet of Beaverkill brown trout serve as an example. Not realizing how fast albacore can run, and their inclination to do so when hooked, I would find myself with the rod tip too high or hand still on the reel handle when a low rod tip and free running reel were indicated.

If the measure of success is to bring the fish you are playing to the net, then any action that allows the fish a measure of lengthening line can be perceived as failure. The farther away the fish moves, the greater the angler's apprehension grows. But, his or her angst may be unwarranted. As long as fish and fisherman remain attached to each other, regardless of the distance that separates them, there is always hope of a successful capture. However, the experience of a fish gaining line as it moves away is most often met with the resolve to stop this from happening. Sooner or later, all but the most experienced fisherman gives ways to his fears and increases the pressure in an often futile attempt to check the fish's run. Doing so increases the strain upon the tippet, and when it becomes too great it breaks. The stunned fisherman turns to his neighbor and utters the classic excuse, "That fish was so big he broke me off." Although you will hear this excuse repeated over and over, don't be misled by its simple logic. Always remember that it is the fisherman who controls the amount of pressure that is applied, and it is he who must modify it as the situation changes. There is a saying at the Wulff school that if you lose a fish but get your fly back it is a "no fault." The cause of this "long-distance release" is attributed to factors beyond the angler's control, such as the failure of the hook to get a good purchase. If, on the other hand, you lose a fish but fail to get your fly back because the tippet broke, the loss is "yo fault."

Conditions can change quickly and often do during the course of fighting a fish. As the fish is brought closer to shore or net, its resolve to escape increases and its movements often become more violent and more unpredictable. The demands on the angler and his equipment also increases under these conditions. A short line offers minimal shock absorbing stretch and significantly reduces the time in which the angler has to react. It is during these last moments of the battle that leaders or lines break and flies lose their hold. Can any of this be avoided? The answer is a definite "yes" for two reasons.

First, being aware of the battle yet to come, the knowing angler plays his fish more gingerly and with less pressure during the early stages of the fight. No need to force the fish into a panic state by applying heavy pressure. The combination of thrashing fish and heavy line pressure can cause the hook to tear flesh and cartilage, which serves to enlarge the size of the hole around it and weaken its grip. Knots also can stretch and weaken under prolonged periods of heavy pressure. Better to conserve any advantage afforded the angler at the time the hook was set and the battle began, than to run the risk of applying too much pressure too early, only to lose the fish at the end of the battle.

Second, knowing that fish will panic the first couple of times that it sees the angler or his net, the angler anticipates the response and reduces line pressure promptly before any harm can be done.

The importance of knowing when and how much pressure to apply can also be seen in the next situation where the fish changes its direction during the fight. Let me begin by asking you to conjure up in your mind the image of a hooked fish with fly firmly implanted in its jaw. Now, let me ask on which side of the fish's jaw did you place the hook, on the side nearest or farthest from yourself?

I will wager that you chose to picture your fish hooked on the side nearest you. With very few exceptions your vision would be accurate. Fish facing upstream will be hooked on the side nearest the angler, and since we know that all fish prefer to face upstream into the oncoming current, the outcome is predictable. So predictable in fact that little thought is ever given to the possibility that the fish you are playing may be hooked on the opposite side of the jaw from which you are playing it. This is not to contradict what has already been said about the fish always facing upstream, and so forth, rather to introduce the concept that as the fish changes its position, the relationship between hook and angler also changes. This change of position occurs, for example, whenever a fish you are playing turns to run downstream or if you are fishing from a boat in still water and the fish crosses beneath you to the other side. A fish initially hooked on the side nearest the angler can very quickly become the fish that is being played from the side facing away from him. The angler must quickly adjust the amount of pressure being applied or risk having the hook pull out and losing the fish.

More pressure can safely be applied when the hook is on the same side as the angler rather than on the side opposite the angler. Under this condition the relationship between the pull of the line and the design of the hook is complementary: pull on the line and the hook digs more deeply. However, when the fish is being played from the side opposite the one it was hooked on, the pull of the line may now be at odds with the design of the hook. The hook shank serves as a lever to dislodge it. Heavy pressure on the line at this time would tend to weaken the hook's grip or pull it free. (See figure 1.3.)

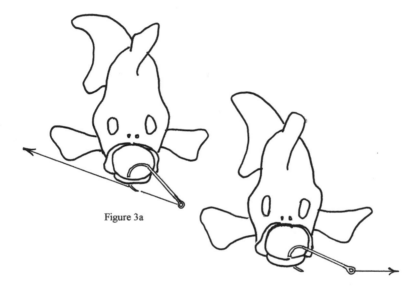

Figure 3a

Figure 3b

Figure 1.3.   Direction of Pull. Figure 1.3a illustrates that when a fish is being played from the side opposite the one it is hooked on, the pull of the line tends to weaken the hold of the hook or to dislodge it altogether. Figure 1.3b illustrates that when a fish is being played from the same side it was hooked on, the pull of the line helps the hook dig more deeply.

When a fish turns to show you its other side, the leader must cross over or under its head or through its mouth. When fighting toothy fish such as pike, barracuda, or mackerel, having the leader pass through the mouth is cause for real concern. Reducing line pressure can help but offers no guarantee against being cut in two. The best insurance lies in using a heavy mono or wire bite guard. (See the "Line/Leader System" section of chapter 3.)

Those who fish still water, be it fresh or salt, are at a disadvantage not knowing on which side their fish is hooked. A momentary glimpse of the fly as the fish jumps or comes close to the surface can answer the question and help tip the scale in the angler's favor. Make it a point to find out as soon as possible on which side your fish is hooked.

When the fish you are playing changes direction and shows you his other side, the odds are with the fish for at least as long as it takes you to adjust line pressure to match the change of conditions. Similarly, when the fish gets in a position below you in moving water, the odds favor the fish. Do you know what to do to improve the odds in your favor?

Greater pressure, and therefore greater strain on equipment, develops when the fish being played moves from upstream of the angler to a position downstream of the angler. In doing so, the need to fight the force of the current's flow is transferred from the fish to the angler. When the fish is upstream of the angler, the fish must fight the force of the current plus any additional force brought to bare by the angler in order to just remain stationary. It is obvious that under these conditions, the angler has the clear advantage. Whenever possible, the wise angler tries to keep downstream of the fish he is playing. The stronger the flow of the current, the more important is the need to do so. But, what do you do if the fish gets below you or was hooked downstream of your position? As you ponder the question, you need to consider who now has the burden of fighting the current and what impact that might have upon your tackle.

If you have ever had to drag a waterlogged stick or glob of moss upstream through heavy current, then you know the effect flowing water has upon an object tethered in its flow. Considerable pressure must be applied just to keep an object stationary. But, what happens if the object is a live fish that you are playing?

The most important consideration is that unlike a stick hanging in the current, a fish can use "hang" time to rest and gain strength. The fisherman, not wanting to let the fish rest, might respond by increasing line pressure in an attempt to draw the fish out of the current or closer to the net, but the results of doing so could prove disastrous. The pressure needed to move the fish upstream against the current allows little margin of safety should the fish turn suddenly and dart downstream in an effort to escape. It is better to use only enough pressure to keep a fish in place while at the same time working to get into a position downstream of it or to use side pressure in an effort to draw the fish out of the current flow, than it is to attempt to drag a fish upstream against the flow.

To this point we have only been talking about when to apply pressure or how much pressure to apply. But, how the pressure is applied can also make a difference. Particularly with regard to a special technique called "walking" a fish.

I still remember standing near the casting pond at the Wulff Fly Fishing School watching bug-eyed in amazement as Lee led or walked a fish first up and then down the shoreline of the casting pond. To do this, he first released all pressure on the line and waited until the fish he had hooked stopped fighting and became stationary. He then moved to a position alongside the fish and very slowly began to apply pressure until the fish began to move. Once the fish was under motion he walked it along the shoreline, being very careful not to change even to the slightest degree the amount of pressure being applied or the speed at which he and the fish were now traveling. At the end of his walk up the shoreline, Lee paused long enough for the fish to settle down. Very carefully he took a new position, this time on the down side of the fish. He applied pressure to tighten the line and very slowly began their walk back down the shoreline.

Perhaps by now your mind is racing ahead and you can identify situations where being able to walk a fish could help you in the future. Two situations will present themselves often enough to warrant mentioning them here. The first is a fish holding at the bottom end or tail-out of a pool. The second situation is a fish holding in heavy water.

A fish that is holding at the tail-out of a pool poses a real threat to the fisherman because of its proximity to an easy escape route. You know what I am talking about. The fish is holding just at the top of the fast water that exits the pool. A couple flips of his tail and the fish, with an angler in tow, is headed downstream for parts unknown. If the angler is unable to follow, start putting the odds on the fish. To keep a fish in the pool and to give yourself a little elbow room in which to play it, try moving the fish nearer to the head of the pool by walking it upstream.

Being able to walk a fish will also come in handy when a fish is holding in heavy water. Remember, as discussed earlier, this situation requires considerable rod pressure just to hold a fish in the current, so the amount of additional pressure that can be applied in playing a fish is very limited. It is usually not so limited, however, as to rule out the possibility of walking a fish out of the current as long as you do it from a position alongside of the fish, not above or below it. So, go ahead, give it a try. I cannot tell you the number of times that I have walked steelhead out of tough places on the Salmon River in upstate New York. Getting a fish out of or keeping it away from strong currents is often the angler's first priority. Walking a fish is one of the safer ways of doing this.

We have seen that pressure can work for or against the angler. In its singular form, that of keeping the same amount of pressure on at all times, the rule works only when playing small fish and is sheer folly when playing big ones. To be of greatest benefit, pressure must be smoothly applied and constantly adjusted when meeting each situation as described: when a fish runs, sulks, gets into fast water, is drawn close to the angler, or radically changes its direction.

Don't Give Any Slack

The worst that can be said about the second rule of playing fish, which is to keep the pressure on, is that it is an oversimplification of the actual process. The worst that could be said about the third rule, which is to never give any slack, is that it is just not good advice. The effective use of slack line when playing a fish is a revolutionary act and perhaps the most important contribution Lee Wulff ever made to fishing. The extent to which slack line can be used to play a fish is truly amazing.

The rationale behind the formulation and long-term acceptance of the no slack rule is the mistaken belief that a fly will lose its hold and fall free of the fish unless held firmly in place by tension on the line. Lose line tension and the hook falls out. It is that simple. The classic magazine cover illustration showing a big fish leaping high into the air, shaking its head violently, and the fly going in the opposite direction is a popular image. The notion that a fish could shake a hook free of its hold is so ingrained in our minds as fishermen that no one bothered questioning its validity. No one, that is, until Lee Wulff found himself confronted by a particularly troublesome set of circumstances.

Early in his career as a filmmaker, Lee was hired by the Canadian Department of Tourism to produce films promoting Atlantic salmon fishing in the Provinces, especially Newfoundland. As it turned out, this was not an easy assignment. Time and time again Lee and his cameraman were caught off guard by the unpredictability of nature, human or otherwise. Hours might pass, for example, from the time Lee started to fish and the camera gear was set in place until a fish was actually hooked. In the meantime light conditions might have changed or nature's call may have sent the cameraman off on his own special mission. Whatever the cause, the results were less than satisfactory film footage of what for many is the greatest thrill of a lifetime, a leaping salmon on the end of line.

In search of a solution, Lee began experimenting with the use of slack line as a way to gain greater control of a hooked fish. Lee reasoned that a fish reacts to being dragged toward shore in much the same way you or I might respond to the act of being dragged toward a dunking in ice water. Should our tormentors stop dragging us, we would stop resisting, preferring instead to save our energy should the changing situation again require it. And, so it is with a hooked fish: take away the offending stimuli and the response to it also goes away. Certain that the hook would not fall out if he took the tension off the line, Lee tested his idea. He tried giving slack line to the fish he hooked and found that they would seek a comfortable spot, usually the same spot it was in when first hooked, and then come to rest. The fish showed little concern for the fly still in their jaw or the slight resistance of the line. Aided with his newfound ability to make fish stop fighting and come to rest, Lee's success at filmmaking soared. As soon as the fish was hooked and then calmed, he and his cameraman would position themselves to their maximum advantage and ready their gear for the action they knew would follow. When everything was at the ready, Lee would tighten the line and the fish, realizing that it was still tethered and fearing for its safety, would come alive and explode out of the water in a grand series of somersaulting leaps. The entire scene was caught on film and later witnessed by thousands of appreciative viewers around the world.

As important as the use of slack line was to Lee's career as a filmmaker, its use as a fish-playing strategy is every bit as important to fishermen. He realized, however, that many would never even give it a try because it runs counter to the notion that if you give line the hook will fall out. He knew that if he was going to be successful in getting his students at the school to at least try slack line techniques when playing fish, he had to overcome this obstacle to learning. Here is how he did it.

Lee challenged anyone who believed that if you give slack line the hook will fall out to do a simple experiment. Take a small fishing fly, with or without a barb, and carefully embed the point of the hook solidly into a fleshy part of your hand. With the fly solidly in place shake your hand as violently as you can in your effort to dislodge it. Fortunately, most are able to foresee the results without having to do the actual experiment; the fly will not fall out.

Do flies ever fall out of fish when you give slack line? Yes, just as they do when you keep the line tight under pressure. There are many reasons why hooks become dislodged, but allowing the line to go slack is, of itself, not one of them. If you can accept that the hook does not automatically fall out if you give slack, then you are in the position to explore using slack line as a way to increase your odds of landing fish under some of the most difficult conditions, conditions that often spell disaster for even experienced anglers.

There are few things that elicit greater panic or despair in the freshwater angler than having a fish he or she is playing tear off downstream in headlong panic, out of the pool, and into the fast water of the next riffle. In the past, the angler would have had few options to consider—chase after the fish in hopes that it would soon stop or increase the pressure in the hope that line, leader, and fly would hold and the fish would be brought to a screeching stop. Let me note here in passing that prayer to some higher authority often accompanies the two approaches. This is as it should be, for neither strategy is all that effective. Fortunately a better strategy now exists, at least for those of you willing to try using slack to your advantage. When I speak of using slack, I don't just mean relaxing pressure on the line, I mean feeding extra line onto the water so as to release as much pressure on the fish as possible. Roll casting a loop of line onto the water is the fastest way to give slack. Do this and be prepared to see your fish stop at the nearest convenient holding spot in the riffle. Amazing! But, it doesn't have to end there. On some occasions when the slack line that you used to stop the fish is allowed to belly in the current below the fish, the fish responds to the pressure from below and moves upstream toward you.

Saltwater anglers use slack line in much the same way as their freshwater counterparts—to stop a fish's panicked run or calm it long enough to allow the angler to take up a better position from which to fight it. If a panicked fish headed downstream into the next riffle or far out to sea is bad scene number one, bad scene number two has got to be the fish that has gotten into a submerged brush pile, rock ledge, or similar obstruction. Any attempt to dislodge such a fish by force usually fails. Thinking back to the earlier analogy of our being dragged toward a vat of ice water and how we would respond, picture a fish that has just been able to make it to the one spot that he knows to be safe from predators only to find that he is being forcefully pulled out of it. What does the fish do? He struggles hard to get free of the force that threatens to pull him from cover and in so doing tangles the line around the snag, breaks the line, and makes good his escape. But what is the angler to do? The key to getting a fish out of cover is to understand why the fish is there in the first place.

A hooked fish seeks refuge because it fears for its safety. After the danger passes, the fish leaves the restricted safety of its sanctuary to resume unrestricted feeding or foraging. The angler's task is to make the fish believe that all is well and it is safe to leave the cover. How better to do this than to take all tension off the line, leader, and fly by giving a little slack line?

If you are patient long enough, you will see the fish leave its sanctuary. The odds are in your favor that when it does, it will follow the same path as went it entered, carrying along with it your line, leader, and fly. Remember that during its life, your fish may have been in and out of this place many times before. Fish are more predictable than we are inclined at first to believe. The wise fisherman is a serious student of fish behavior.

Figure 1.4 shows my friend and expert angler Gordy Hill of Big Pine Key, Florida, with an Australian barramundi, which he caught over a rocky flat. Three times the fish fought his way to the safety of the rocks. Three times he gave slack and waited. Three times the fish fell for the trick and had to fight its way back to safety, but

Figure 1.4. Gordon Hill with an Australian barramundi that he caught over a rocky flat. Three times the fish fought its way to safety in the rocks. Three times he gave slack and each time the fish fell for the trick, leaving the rocks and having to do battle once more.

each time with less resolve. Finally, with its store of energy at a low level, it gave up.

The notion that fish can be engaged psychologically as well as physically is not new. It has been around for a long time, as suggested in the very way we choose to describe the act of catching a fish. Throughout this book I use "playing fish" and "fighting fish" interchangeably, as is the custom. However, my natural inclination is to use "playing a fish" whenever reason directs the action, and "fighting a fish" whenever brawn prevails. Lee Wulff did not invent this psychological approach to playing fish, but was a serious student of this subject. He combined his knowledge of fish behavior and slack line technique to develop a strategy that has come to change how I now view fighting fish.

The common thread that runs throughout the many uses of slack line is the calming effect it has on a fish. This can serve the angler well anytime he is confronted with a situation that requires time. Once, for example, while playing a salmon in Newfoundland, Lee was faced with a reel that was about to seize up and stop turning. Quickly he stripped off enough line necessary to take all the tension off the fish and it settled calmly behind a rock in the middle of the river. Then Lee tied the line to a branch of a nearby alder and proceeded to drive the six miles back to the inn at which he was staying to get another reel. Returning to the fish, he cut the line and attached it to the new reel. When everything was in order, he tightened the line and the fight was on. How big was the salmon? Eighteen pounds!

Having heard Lee's fish-playing lecture many times at the school, I was well acquainted with it but felt that I was never in a good situation to try putting it to practice. One day, as fate would have it, I hooked a particularly nice colored brown trout of about twenty-one inches in length and was planning to take a picture of it. It was then that I discovered that I had left my camera back in the truck, which was parked a couple hundred yards away. What a perfect opportunity, I thought, to put Lee's lesson to the test. I followed his example to a T. I gave slack to calm the fish, laid my rod on the ground, and, fearing the fish might drag it off, took my vest off and put it on top of the rod. I hurried back to my truck, retrieved my camera, and headed back to where the fish was.

The line had drifted well downstream in a big U. My heart sunk. I hurried over the stony shore to where the rod lay. I was concerned about the large amount of line that was on the water and the pressure it would add if the battle with the fish got serious. Carefully I picked up the rod and began walking downstream, reeling in the loop of line as I went. By the time I had walked twenty feet I had taken in most of the slack and for the first time could feel that the fish was still there. Just then I realized that my net was on my vest and the vest lay where I had put in when I covered the rod. With only a moment's hesitation, I laid the rod down once more, hurried to the vest, putting it on as I returned to the rod. Because of my decision to walk downstream of the fish while it was holding still, the contest was decided quickly in my favor. The fish was landed and a photo taken. Thanks Lee!

You may not ever find yourself in either of the situations above, but I would bet money on the belief that sooner or later you will find yourself in a situation where you will need some extra time. Perhaps it will be time to get out of a boat, to reposition yourself along the beach for greater maneuverability, or to adjust your tackle. There are many situations that often need to be taken care of at the time you are least wanting to do so. I mean like when you have hooked the biggest fish of your life and your reel falls off. Use slack line to calm your fish and buy the time you need. My first experience was a success. I hope yours will be a success as well.

Having now completed an in-depth review and analysis of slack line as a fish-fighting technique, our investigation of the three rules of playing fish is finished. In their original form, when presented as strict rules to be followed without exception, these rules are of limited value. Follow them and you are destined to lose most if not all of the exceptional fish you hook. But, when viewed as a place from which to start, the three rules offer valuable information for anyone willing to invest the time to separate the wheat from the chaff. That is, for anyone willing to learn the rules and learn when to break them as we have done.

TWO

A MODERN APPROACH

The three rules of playing fish discussed in chapter 1 evolved over time and were transmitted from one generation of anglers to another. These rules can be seen as reflecting what anglers of the past saw as being the most important considerations when playing fish. Keeping the rod tip up to provide shock protection, not allowing slack so as to provide the line tension needed to keep the hook from falling out of the fish's mouth, and keeping the pressure on to tire the fish, making it work harder as it tried to escape. We can conclude, therefore, that a desire to keep fish and fisherman connected and to tire the fish sufficiently in order to bring it to net were central concerns. As time went on, however, careful observers such as Lee Wulff were finding the rules wanting and at times in conflict with one another. Rather than always keeping the rod high, for example, it is important to lower the rod tip and reduce pressure when a fish runs to avoid breaking it off. So, exceptions to the rules had to be made as situations demanded. Although Lee Wulff was a significant contributor to our present-day list of rule exceptions, I do not believe that he was playing by the rules at all. Rather he used his knowledge of the rules to get and keep control of the fish so he could better manage the fight on his terms. This focus on control is one of two key elements in today's enlightened approach to playing fish.

A fish is said to be under control when the fisherman determines in which direction the fish moves. Since a fish moves in the direction its head is pointed, control the head and you control the fish.

Control can be direct or indirect. Pull a fish toward you or lift it to the surface and the control is direct. If a fish moves in the direction you want it to as the result of, or in response to, something you have done other than pulling it, the control is indirect. Examples of indirect control would be to calm a fish by giving it slack line or to move a fish upstream by putting a belly of line in the current below. As a general rule, direct control carries the greatest risk of break off, hence, is reserved for small fish or at the end of the battle when the fish is tired.

The most common indirect control position and the one used to tire a fish most efficiently places the fish facing and pulling away from the angler with its head being held above the level of its tail. In moving water, this position would also require that the fish be upstream of the angler. The line should be running parallel along the fish's side when the fish is surging straight ahead. If the fish is turning, the line is placed at a low angle on the side opposite the turn.

When playing a large fish, the first objective is to get control and maintain it as long as possible. The success of doing this is greatly influenced by the angler's ability to recognize when he or she is not in control and how to use this knowledge of the rules to counter the fish's moves in order to regain control once lost. The application of rules, once thought of as the main objective, now takes on a different, more supporting role, serving as the means to the end rather than the end itself.

The true-to-life fish-fighting example that follows will help you to better understand today's modern approach to playing big fish. The hook is set! The fish, a beautiful Atlantic salmon of about twenty pounds, is startled and in utter panic. It races upstream, leaping and twisting as it tries to outdistance its perceived pursuer. The angler lowers his rod tip to reduce the tension on the line by decreasing the friction caused as the line races through the guides. The panic of the hook set subsides and the fish slows. Applying hand pressure to the rim of the reel, the angler slowly increases the drag, and in so doing, increases the burden now being placed upon the fish. The fish must work even harder now to put distance between them. The angler raises his rod tip slightly in an effort to gain some shock protection against the sudden maneuver he knows is coming. The strain on the fish grows intolerable and perhaps hoping to shake its unknown burden, it turns suddenly and rushes downstream. Control for the angler is lost. The angler swings his rod tip downstream in an attempt to get his line ahead of the fish and lead it toward himself. The maneuver worked and for a time the fish is headed straight toward the angler. The angler takes up the slack line and once again is in control. The fish abruptly changes direction again and flees downstream. The angler, a well-seasoned veteran, had anticipated this move and almost as quickly as it was executed by the fish, he stops reeling in line, takes his hand off the reel handle, lowers his rod tip, and lets the fish run against the light preset drag. The fish is now in control and there is little for the angler to do but follow it downstream in an effort to keep it as close as possible. The angler changes the angle of his rod tip, holding it low and to his downstream side, hoping to make the fish lose its balance enough to cause it to turn. The distance between fish and angler is too great, and the maneuver fails to achieve sufficient side pressure to change the fish's direction. Short of breath and tired from running after the fish, the angler grows concerned knowing that there is but little backing left on his reel. "If I do not stop this fish soon," he thinks to himself, "I will lose it."

Fearing that any additional pressure that he might apply in an attempt to stop the fish would cause the tippet to break, the angler quickly strips backing off the reel, adding the slack onto the water. The fish, sensing this release of pressure, turns to take a position below a midstream boulder that serves to block the heavy flow. Its mouth and gills working together to add oxygen to a system depleted in the fish's downstream dash. Thankful that the tactic was successful in stopping the fish, the angler now moves farther downstream toward the holding fish, taking in precious backing as he walks. Nervously the fish changes position, slipping downstream in the current whenever a misstep causes the angler to stumble, sending a telltale signal to the fish that the danger has not passed. It is a standoff, line gained is soon lost. With the fish downstream of the angler, it is the fish that has the advantage. The fisherman cannot hope to drag the fish up through the fast water. The additional weight created by the pressure of the water against the fish would surely break the light tippet if he attempted to do so. But, neither can he afford to let the fish rest and gain strength. In a bold gamble to gain control, the angler once again gives slack line; this time his plan is different. He will use the slack to position a portion of the line below the fish. He feeds slack line onto the water until there is enough line to cause considerable drag once it has stopped and is allowed to belly below the fish. The gamble works, the fish responds to the line pressure from below as if the danger is now coming from behind. The fish surges upstream past the angler, tailing behind it the belly of line that it now wants to escape. As the fish passes the angler he quickly recovers as much line as possible before the fish gets too far upstream. With most of the belly removed, the line tightens as the fish continues to move upstream. The angler realizes that it is now he, not the fish, that is in control. He lifts his rod tip and adds more drag pressure using his palm against the rim of the reel spool to make the tiring fish work even harder. The fish responds to the demands placed upon its failing strength by turning and heading downstream once more. The angler's response is quick in coming. He swings his rod tip downstream to position the line ahead of the fish and leads it toward himself. The fish tries to turn away, the attempt is but a futile gesture showing the depth of its exhaustion and the loss of the will to fight. Carefully the angler readies his net and draws the fish nearer. The fish, startled by the decreasing depth of the water and the feeling of gravel on its belly, panics and with every ounce of strength remaining, turns and heads for deeper water. The angler lowers his rod tip and points it directly at the fleeing fish. Fortunately for the angler, the run is a short one and in no time at all he is able to gain control, with the fish above him facing upstream with the line close to its side. Not wanting to repeat the situation that almost cost him the fish, the angler moves out from where he has been standing to take a position in deeper water before turning the fish and bringing it once more toward the waiting net. With fish and mouth of the net on a collision course, the angler lowers his rod tip to release the tension on the line so it will not be broken when it comes in contact with the net. With the fish safely in the net, the angler carefully removes the hook, takes the fish from the net to cradle it in his hands, and then watches as it swims away.

Of those few anglers who do ascribe to the more modern control approach, most still view it as a way to tire a fish so it can be successfully brought to the net. However, there is yet one more important element in our modern approach that goes beyond using control to tire a fish. This is the acceptance of the belief that a fish has not only the ability to fight or not fight as the limits of its physical strength allows, but is endowed with the will to fight or to surrender to its fate.

I am sure that every experienced fisherman has at one time or another encountered the situation where a fish he is playing falls far short of his expectations for a strong fight. It is as if at some point the fish simply decided to give up. At first I attributed this kind of behavior to physical causes such as the location of the hook deep in the mouth or throat or the fact that the fish had become tangled in the line. However, information collected over the years has failed to support such claims. I now believe the explanation lies in the knowledge that every animal has limits not only to its physical endurance but to its psychological endurance as well. Any wild animal tethered on a leash for the first time will pull out all the stops trying to escape. But, when biting, twisting, and pulling fails to free it, the animal finally comes to accept its condition and loses its will to fight. And so it is with fish. The most dramatic example of fish giving up their will to fight that I have witnessed happened at the Sunnybrook Trout Club near Sandusky, Ohio.

I was at Sunnybrook to conduct a fly fishing school for some of its members. While there I took advantage of the invitation to fish its beautiful spring creek. I had hooked and landed two nice trout but while attempting to land the third, it came off the hook as it was passing through the mat of vegetation that grew near the shore. Almost completely surrounded by the thick mat, it lay motionless even though it was free of the hook. Concerned with its welfare, I reached down, removed it from the vegetation, and scooted it into open water. It took off without the slightest hesitation. When the same incident repeated itself a little later, my attention was drawn to it. I mentioned the incidents to my coinstructor and he too reported having had a similar experience. Afterward I recalled witnessing similar behavior when frantically struggling fish give up once captured and lifted from the water in a net. If not loss of the will to fight, how else do we explain this phenomenon that causes strong fresh fish to suddenly go limp and cease to struggle?

Lee Wulff was one who believed it possible to break a fish of its will to fight if the angler could foil each and every attempt the fish made to make good its escape. This is extremely hard to do although I have had it happen more by chance and good fortune than skill on my part. Fortunately, even when control is incomplete, shifting from fish to angler and back again, the fish's will to fight can still be engaged and hopefully defeated.

Contests for control that occur between fish and angler in the course of the fight are not equal in their importance. Some happen so quickly and indecisively that they pass with little notice, while others, those of longer duration and highly contested, deserve notice. These confrontational episodes are extremely important because they involve the fish's will to fight and allow us the opportunity to wage a battle on two fronts—the physical and the psychological. Win one of these confrontational battles of the will and you increase the likelihood that the will becomes less combative and easier to bring to the net. This was the case with a trevalle I had hooked off a reef in Christmas Island.

CHAPTER TWO

As soon as I set the hook, the fished headed over the reef and to the bottom of the lagoon. I held on, applying all the pressure I dared. A stalemate developed and continued for several minutes. The fish was stopped short of the bottom, and try as it might the fish could go no farther. I was bound and determined to keep it from doing so. My goal now was not so much to tire the fish as it was to take away its will to fight. To be successful, I knew I needed to win the tug-of-war that had developed between us. The fish kept pulling straight ahead and I held my ground. Then, like an animal on a rope, it gave up and stopped trying, far short of its limits of physical endurance. The battle was over. A word of caution is in order here. Fish that are still fresh in a physical sense, although lacking the will to fight, are capable of explosive reactions when a landing is attempted; be prepared to act quickly to avoid breaking them off or doing harm to yourself or the fish.

Our approach to playing fish has evolved and changed over the years. As discussed in chapter 1, we were at first guided by a set of three rules and their many exceptions. Our approach to fighting fish was to keep the pressure on it in order to tire it and rob it of its ability to resist. Only then could it be brought safely to the net. Today our approach is to gain and keep control of the fish and to land it whenever an opportunity to do so presents itself. Our concept of control has also been broadened to include both physical and psychological aspects. To break a fish of its will to fight is to achieve mastery over it without having to first deny it of its strength to do so. This is especially important when fighting tarpon and other large saltwater fish. To get and stay in control of a fish requires that the angler successfully counter every move the fish makes in its effort to make good its escape. For the fish it is a matter of physical strength, conditioned response, and its will to fight. For the fisherman, it is a matter of responding most appropriately to each situation, making full use of his intelligence, past experiences, and knowledge of the rules and techniques for playing fish. As you learn more about these techniques, it is important to remember that they all share one thing in common: they work best when the fish is near, within twenty feet or so of the angler. A long line not only makes applied side pressure less effective, it introduces line stretch, which robs the angler of vital feedback, often too little too late. A long line also increases the risk of getting hooked on a snag and adds unwanted drag on the line itself. When playing a fish, closer is better.

THREE

BEYOND THE RULES— EQUIPMENT

Selection of equipment may take place days or months prior to being used. Nevertheless, your ability to play fish most effectively will be influenced by these choices. Taking the time to become familiar with the many equipment options available and how each might work for or against you will yield significant dividends, and could even save you money in the process.

Rods

We begin our exploration of fishing equipment with a look at the rod as a fish-fighting tool. In this same light, but later in this chapter, we shall also explore the characteristics of reels, lines, and leaders.

A fishing rod serves to cast the line and fly plus acts as a shock absorber when playing fish. The terms fast or slow action describe a rod's casting characteristics. A rod that is quick to load (stiffens sufficiently under compression to be able to cast the line) is said to be "fast" or to have a "fast action." A rod that takes longer to load is said to be "slow" or to have a "slow action." Terms such as flexibility or stiffness are used to describe a rod's ability to bend or flex under stationary or static conditions. It is this property that is the focus of our attention.

Stiffness is determined by the rod's design (i.e., the thickness of the walls and the material it is made of). Fishing rods that are soft and full flexing, those that bend deeply from tip to butt, are generally best for fighting fish. Unfortunately, bending characteristics are difficult to describe with any precision. Every rod company has its own idea of what constitutes a soft rod or a stiff one, so it is difficult to make cross-company comparisons. What is lacking is an industry-wide standard by which all rods are judged and their stiffness described. The Orvis Company of Manchester, Vermont, has taken a big step forward in this regard with the use of a static deflection technique to establish a flex index ranging from 2.5 to 12.5. Rods classified, for example, as full flex (2.5 to 5.5) all share the same flexural characteristics and can be relied upon to yield similar performance. Until this or a similar system is standardized and accepted for use by all, we are left to rely upon rod manufacturer's descriptions and our own field experiences. Figure 3.1 shows rod flex profiles for the three most common flex categories: full flex, mid flex, and tip flex. For a more accurate and versatile way to describe and compare the flex characteristics of rods you have, you can make your own stiffness profiles by tracing the curvature of the rod when it is under tension. You can then use the tracing to compare it to the stiffness profiles of other rods you might wish to purchase. Figure 3.2 shows a diagram of a rod tracing setup.

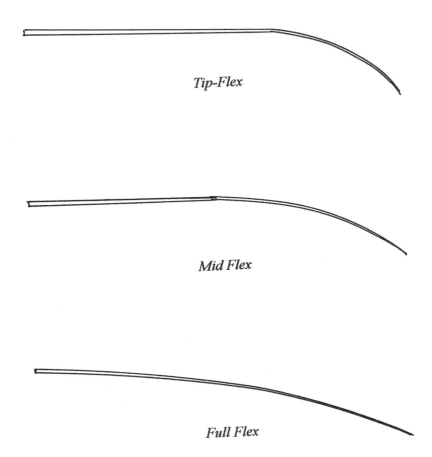

Tip-Flex

Mid Flex

Full Flex

Figure 3.1.   Rod Flex Diagram

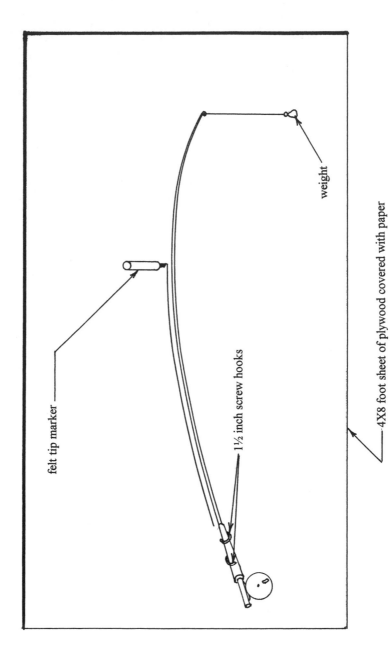

felt tip marker

1½ inch screw hooks

weight

4X8 foot sheet of plywood covered with paper

Figure 3.2. Rod Tracing Diagram

To make a tracing you need two one-and-a-half-inch screw hooks, a sheet of 4x8-foot plywood, and a roll of white wrapping paper. Cover the plywood with the paper and attach the rod at the handle and reel seat along one side using the two screw hooks to hold the rod in position against the paper. Place the plywood against the wall and attach weight to the line of the strung rod, allowing the weight to hang down about a foot from the tip guide. The amount of the weight should be ten times the weight in grains of the line recommended by manufacture for the rod being tested. For example, the proper weight for a six weight rod would be 160 grains times 10 or 1,600 grains. See table 3.1 to convert line weight to weight in grains. Since I do not have a grain scale, I use a combination of U.S. coins to meet weight requirements. For example, when profiling six weight rods, I use 17 quarters, 1 nickel, and 1 dime. Each quarter weighs 87.65 grains, the nickel 75.35 grains, and the dime 34.6 grains. A penny weighs 38.75 grains.

Once the appropriate weight has been attached to the line, the shape of the bent rod can now be traced

Table 3.1. **Fly Line Standards of the American Tackle Manufacturer's Association**

Code	Weight/Grains
1	60
2	80
3	100
4	120
5	140
6	160
7	185
8	210
9	240
10	280
11	330
12	380

using a felt tip marker and the tracings used to compare rods. Using this variable weight system allows for more accurate comparison of profiles between rods of differing weights. For example, you can compare the profile of your favorite five weight with an eight weight you might consider buying.

Every rod stiffens under compression and at some point becomes rigid and no longer acts as a good shock absorber. With this in mind, you might wish to gradually add weight on the rod tip in order to determine at what point the rod loses its ability to flex. With this information you will be better able to balance the shock absorbing limits of the rod to the size of the fish you will most likely encounter. It is kind of like matching the rod to the fish. The following example will show what I mean.

For many years I fished the Connecticut River near the Holyoke dam for American shad. The water was fast moving and the fish were in the five- to eight-pound range. Most of the time I would use a soft, nine-foot, seven weight fly rod to handle the situation. On one particular occasion my curious nature took over my better judgment and I decided to fish with a six-foot ultra-light spinning outfit. What I thought would be fun proved to be totally impractical and not the least bit fun. Almost as soon as the fish was hooked it was lost. Bent almost double and close to breaking, the rod became as inflexible as a broomstick, affording no shock protection at all. The light pressure that the rod was capable of exerting on the fish before becoming rigid was far below what was needed to play the fish in the fast current. A good fish-fighting rod needs to be flexible over a wide range of line tension. Knowing the useful limits of your rods will help you select the best rod for each situation you encounter. When fishing in fast water, for example, it is helpful to use a rod rated one or two line sizes above the one you might use to fish for the same or comparable fish species in a lake or

Table 3.2.   Recommended Rod/Line Weights for Popular Game Fish

Bass (Freshwater)	7–9
Bluefish/Striped Bass/Albacore	7–9
Flat Fish (Bonefish, Permit, Snook, etc.)	6–10
Pan Fish (Perch, Bluegills, Crappie, etc.)	3–6
Pike/Muskellunge	7–9
Redfish	7–9
Sailfish/Marlin (and other offshore species)	9–15
Sharks	10–15
Steelhead/Salmon (Atlantic and Pacific)	6–10
Trout/Shad	3–7

small stream. Remember, the objective is to select a rod that affords maximum shock absorbency throughout the full range of anticipated stresses your fishing situation might present. Table 3.2 gives recommended rod/line sizes for common game fish under usual fishing conditions common to the species.

When properly matched to conditions, the rod acts as both a shock absorber and a lever, affording the angler a measure of protection against shock while at the same time providing sufficient backbone to lever a fish when it is necessary to do so. While it is easy to understand how the rod functions as a shock absorber, the rod's function as a lever can be confusing even to experts as the following example shows.

During the course of a discussion expounding the virtues of using long rods of ten to fourteen feet in length to land large fish on light leaders, a noted steelhead fisherman said, "Basically it is a law of physics. The longer the lever, the greater the pressure/work that can be applied/completed."

The lever advantage of the long rod is a common misconception. Actually the lever advantage goes to the fish not the fisherman. The shorter the rod the easier it is to apply pressure. That is why rods used to handle really big fish like tuna are quite short, five to six feet in length. What the expert quoted above did not understand was that when bent almost double, his long noodle rod functioned as if it were a short rod. When it comes to rod length the functional or effective length is more important than its physical length. The functional length is described as the distance between two imaginary lines, one running from the tip of the rod to the fish and the other running parallel to it but passing along the top of the rod handle. (See figure 3.3.)

While functional length is not a rod characteristic per se, it can be the direct result of one, namely, rod stiffness. The more flexible the rod, the more readily it will bend, making it easier to apply force than with a stiffer rod of the same length and line weight.

Bending a rod is not, however, the only way to change its functional length. Decreasing the rod-to-fish angle, that angle between an imaginary line running from the rod handle and the fish and a second imaginary line running parallel along the handle of the rod, will also produce similar results without relying on rod flexibility. This is easily accomplished by pointing the rod more directly at the fish. When the rod is pointed directly at the fish, the rod-to-fish angle is zero degrees, and there is no lever effect to subtract from the force exerted by the angler. Thus maximum force can be applied.

There is still another way to change the functional length of a rod and that is to grasp the shaft of the rod a foot or so up the rod with the second or line hand. The distance between the hand nearest the rod tip and the rod tip itself is now the measure of the rod's functional length. Some heavy duty saltwater rods are equipped with a second handle mounted in place. This serves as notice of the rod's intended use, one for which it was designed and built. To use the second hand on rods not specifically designed for this purpose requires careful execution. When the second hand

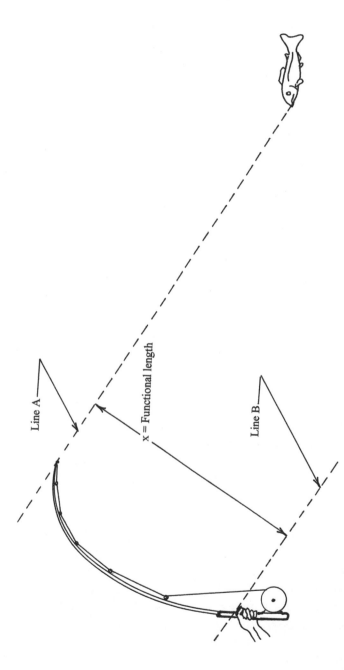

Figure 3.3. **Functional Rod Length. The functional length (x) is described as the distance between two imaginary lines, one running from the tip of the rod to the fish (line A) and the other running parallel to it but passing along the top of the rod hand (line B).**

is used only to relieve the rod hand from having to do all the work and affording it some time to rest, there is little danger of breaking the rod as long as the amount of pressure being exerted does not increase. When the use of the second hand is employed as a means of adding additional pressure rather than just gaining some needed resting time, the situation can get out of hand quickly. The use of the second hand blocks the flex of the rod, adding disproportionate flex elsewhere. The use of the second hand also makes it possible for the angler to apply even greater force than with just one hand alone, thanks to the lever advantage the rod hand now enjoys. Combine these two outcomes—disproportionate flex and the ability to apply even greater force—and the odds are that a rod is going to get broken. When using the second hand hold, the amount of pressure being exerted can skyrocket far beyond what most rods can handle. Use great care when using the two-handed technique to apply additional pressure.

Up until now rod length and shock absorbency have been treated as if they were separate and unrelated variables. This is not the case. It is important to understand that while changing the rod-to-fish angle changes functional length, it also changes how the rod functions as a shock absorber. Shock absorbency and application of pressure are opposites along a continuum. As the rod-to-fish angle increases, shock absorbency increases but one's ability to apply pressure decreases. (See figure 3.4.)

The challenge when playing a fish is to maintain adequate pressure to control and tire a fish while at the same time providing adequate protection from shock. The rod handling techniques used to maintain this fine balance will depend on the length and flexibility of the rod. In general, long flexible rods such as noodle and Spey rods work best when flexed deeply beyond ninety degrees. Shorter, stiffer rods, on the other hand, work best at angles less than ninety degrees.

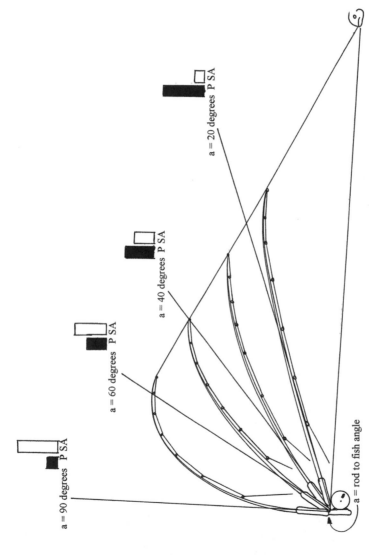

a = 20 degrees P SA

a = 40 degrees P SA

a = 60 degrees P SA

a = 90 degrees P SA

a = 60 degrees

a = 40 degrees

a = rod to fish angle

Figure 3.4.   The Relationship of Rod Pressure to Shock Absorbency. As the rod/fish angle (a) increases, shock absorbency (SA) increases as the ability to apply pressure (P) decreases.

I would encourage you to take some time and explore the relationship between force and shock protection. Be careful, however, not to overstress the rod causing it to break. As the rod-to-fish angle increases, stress that was distributed along the full length of the rod becomes more concentrated at a limited area along its shaft. When over-flexing causes excessive stress on the fragile tip section breakage can occur.

Overstressing the rod tip is a common cause of rod breakage while playing a fish. The situation occurs when the angler fails to take the pressure off the tip as the fish is brought nearer and nearer. When the fish is forty or fifty feet from the angler, the ninety-degree hold places the stress on the stronger midsection of the rod. The same ninety-degree hold when the fish is six or seven feet from the angler causes stress to be focused on the more fragile tip section. It is here that the breakage most often occurs, the combination of an overstressed rod and the lunge of a desperate fish. (See figure 3.5.)

To relieve the stress on the rod tip as the fish is brought to the net, the angler needs to turn his wrist rearward and shove the rod back to position the butt of the rod as far away from the fish as possible. (See figure 3.6.) When netting a fish, you will also find that shorter, more flexible rods are desirable. It is, for example, almost impossible for the lone angler using a rather stiff twelve- or fourteen-foot Euro or Spey rod to net his own fish. Beaching a fish or repositioning the rod hand several feet up on the rod shaft to reduce its length are the only options available to the lone angler.

Rod length and stiffness are characteristics that are important to our attempts to maintain an optimum balance between rod pressure and shock protection. Achieving this balance, however, requires more than that knowledge. It requires hands-on experience as well. The drawing in figure 3.7 shows a device that can be used to explore

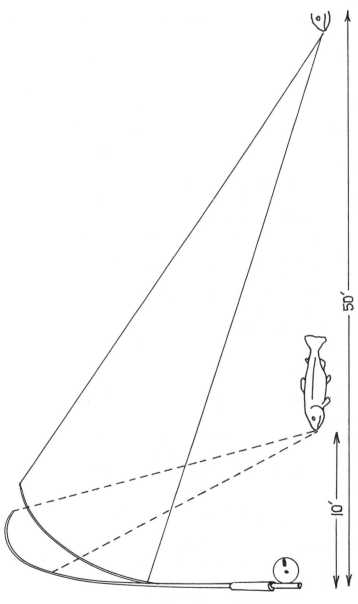

50'

10'

Figure 3.5. **Rod Stress Distribution. Stress on the rod is concentrated in the tip section as the fish is drawn closer to the angler.**

Figure 3.6. **To relieve the stress on the rod tip as the fish is brought to the net, the angler needs to extend his hand behind himself to position the butt of the rod as far away from the fish as possible.**

Joan Wulff Photo

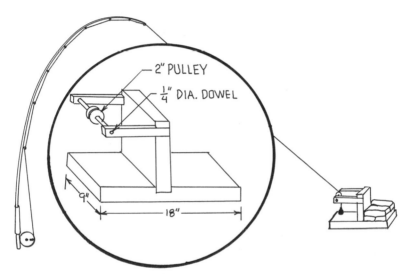

Figure 3.7.   A Mechanical "Fish" Practice Device

further how the rod functions as a fish-fighting tool. It is especially helpful for practicing how to apply pressure under changing conditions such as when the rod tip is held high, pointed directly at the "fish," or with the "fish" close or far away. One of my favorite exercises is to keep the weight suspended in one place as I raise the rod tip. To do this successfully requires that the loss of the rod's lifting force, which results as the rod tip is raised, be compensated for by adding additional hand and arm force. Don't get it right and the weight rises or falls dramatically, causing the kind of shock to the line/leader system that can cause a fish to break off. Practice makes perfect!

Reels

Let me introduce this section with a scenario meant to reveal the kinds of problems often encountered when fish are being fought. Imagine that you are using a spring and pawl or click drag system on a seven weight light saltwater reel. You set the reel's drag for two pounds, more than enough to keep the spool from overrunning. You later decide to add a couple more pounds of drag to help tire the fish, something to make him work harder. The drag is now set for four pounds. On the hook set, the fish suddenly turns ninety degrees and races off across the flats. Line tension soars upward from four to six pounds as the drag is engaged. When the effects of the startup are overcome and the reel is turning smoothly, line tension is reduced. As the fish takes out more line, line tension once again begins to increase. As each layer of line is removed from the reel spool, the effective diameter of the spool grows smaller. Now with perhaps all the fly line off the reel the spool size may be reduced by as much as one-half its starting diameter. The amount of line tension now needed to take line off the reel has doubled, going from four pounds to eight. Assuming that you are using a ten-pound tippet, the margin of safety between drag setting and the breaking strength of line or tippet is compromised and there is little margin for error. The straw that will break the camel's back is about to be added. The ninety or so feet of fly line that went zinging off the reel on the fish's first long run is now being pulled through the water. The weight of that line plus the resistance or drag of the water against it is all that is needed to break the tippet. One way to help cut our losses is to have more information with which to better evaluate, select, and use our reels as a fish-fighting tool.

All fishing reels share one thing in common—they store line. The characteristic design differences that separate the spinning reels, plug casting reels, and fly reels is a function of how the line is to be stored. The spinning reel stores line on a drum positioned parallel to the line as it enters and exits the reel. Plug casting and fly reels store line on spools that are perpendicular to the line as it enters and exits the reel. Although similar in this regard, the line on the fly reel must be pulled off by hand before being cast while the line on the plug casting reel comes off automatically with the cast. This feature of plug casting reels necessitates the need for two separate drag systems—one to control spool overrun when casting and the other drag system for playing fish. Fly reels, as you will discover later, have only one drag system.

When the three reel types are viewed in terms of their function as a place to store line, the amount of line that can be stored becomes a major variable, dictating as it does a wide variety of reel sizes within each reel type. The size of the arbor on which the line is wound has received considerable attention in recent years from fly fishermen and reel designers and will be discussed later at length. However, any spin fisher will tell you that a quality drag system is the single most important factor determining the number of fish landed to those lost.

Most freshwater fly fishers of my generation see the reel as simply a place to store line. Any drag that might be present serves to prevent spool overrun. In the evolution of the fly reel, it was the demand of saltwater anglers for reels with drags strong enough to tire long running species such as albacore and tuna that prompted reel designers and manufacturers to produce reels that could actually help anglers land their catches. To function in this manner, these reels had to possess drag systems that could be adjusted through a wide range of tension and provide smooth, nonjerky startups. Some of the more sophisticated reels also included an antireverse feature that allows the reel handle to remain stationary and under the angler's direct control as the line is going off the reel. When combined, these two features create an extremely effective fish-fighting reel, no longer just a place to store line. Many experienced anglers of both fresh and salt water, however, still prefer direct drive reels with minimal drag systems, choosing to manually apply extra drag that might be needed. Regardless of which reel you select to use, your choice will have an impact on your later fish-playing successes. It is, therefore, very important that you know the fish-fighting advantages and disadvantages for the features on the reels you have or may wish to purchase in the future.

Drag system, drive system, and arbor size have already been identified as being important. What follows is a closer look as to how each directly impacts your ability to play a fish from the reel.

As mentioned earlier, the drag system is the single most important feature when choosing a reel. Drags come in two basic types—spring and pawl and friction plates. The latter can be further divided into three groups, those that use multiple discs, those that use a disc and caliper system similar to the disc brakes on an automobile, and the newer cone type recently introduced by the Waterworks Company of Ketchum, Idaho.

Reels designed around the spring and pawl drag are extremely popular for light freshwater trout fishing. These reels offer simplicity, light weight, and economy. Their greatest shortcoming is their high startup resistance. This startup inertia, as the resistance is often called, represents the combined force of inertia (a body at rest tends to stay at rest) and friction. The friction is the result of the resistance of the pawl spring against the pawl. As the pawl moves over each tooth on the gear drive, it rises against the pawl spring and then falls into the valley between each tooth. Moments of increased friction are followed by moments of none. The interrupted click, click, click that spring and pawl reels makes gives voice to the irregular drag they produce. Over the years I have used dozens of these reels on as many fish species. Just thinking about using one and imagining a fish taking off from a dead stop against an engaged drag makes me hold my breath. If the leader is going to break or the hook pull out this would be the time for it to happen. The greater the line tension on the startup, the greater the risk of losing fish.

Startup resistance is present to some degree with all reels. However, reels with friction systems are able to keep it to a minimum since the friction is uniform between drag components. This is especially true of drags that rely on multiple plates or a cone rather than the disc and caliper to generate braking power. If you are curious about how well your reel's drag is performing, and I hope you are, try the simple tests described below.

A quick and easy way to determine drag performance, especially startup resistance and smoothness of operation, begins with the reel in one hand and the line held in the other. The hand holding the line adjusts the drag setting to the point where when you let the reel fall from your hand, it slowly descends to the floor. If the setting is too light, the reel will hit the floor and fall over. If the reel descends slowly enough to allow the reel to touch down lightly and remain standing on the rim rather than falling over on its side, the setting is correct. Testing can now begin.

To get a better understanding of startup resistance and to what extent it is present in the reel being tested, begin to add smooth steady tension on the line to lift the reel off the floor. This lifting of the reel demonstrates startup resistance. To determine the strength of this resistance begin a series of trials in which you carefully increase the speed of the lift. To get some reels turning, a jerk on the line strong enough to catapult the reel into the air will be required. Reels with the smoothest operating drags and the least startup resistance will allow you to pull fifteen or twenty feet of line off the reel without it tipping over or lifting it off the ground. The faster you can start the line moving without this happening, the better. Becoming familiar with how well your reel functions under different conditions gives you a special advantage when playing a fish.

The reel's drag system can be used when fighting a fish by providing extra pressure on the line. In the fish's efforts to get away it must fight against this pressure and in doing so it tires itself to a point that the angler gains the upper hand. This sounds easy but as you saw in the fishing scenario at the beginning of this section, it is not. Tension on the line is never constant for any length of time, changing as conditions change. Raise the rod tip, for example, and tension on the line increases. The fish changes direction and darts away and line tension increases. Because there are dozens of conditions that can dramatically increase or decrease line tension and because they have a tendency to present themselves in rapid succession, no one drag setting can be expected to cover the entire spectrum of need. Drags are, therefore, usually set for one of two purposes—to prevent the spool from overrunning or to help fight the fish. While both types of drag systems can do either job adequately, friction type reels are better suited for fighting fish from the reel. Many of our more experienced saltwater fishermen prefer only enough drag to prevent overrunning.

To set a drag for the purpose of preventing overrun, put the drag on its lowest setting and then increase it slowly to the point where a hard jerk on the line causes the reel to turn and the line to unspool easily but not in excess. You can check this adjustment by holding the reel in one hand and the line in the other. Move your hands apart as quickly as you can, being careful not to interfere with the reel's function. Separate them about three feet, then stop abruptly. If the line between the reel and your hand is straight, the tension is too much. If the line between the reel and the line hand sags more than one foot, the setting is too light. (See figure 3.8.) Lefty Kreh suggests holding the fly line between your dry lips and adjusting the drag to match that amount of tension. I tried doing this and found the resulting drag setting to be just shy of two pounds.

Some anglers, especially among those who fish fresh water, prefer to use a little extra drag that they use to tire a fish more quickly than one adjusted just to preventing overrunning. When the drag is to be used in this manner, it is customary to set it to equal one quarter of the rated breaking strength of the tippet to be used. If, for example, you are using twelve-pound tippet, set the drag for three pounds. This is easily done with a spring scale. However, you can arrive at about the same setting by replacing the scale with a short piece of tippet material with a known breaking strength equal to the drag setting desired, or about three pounds in this example. Attach one end of the tippet to a solid object like a doorknob and the other to the line coming from the reel. Starting from a point of

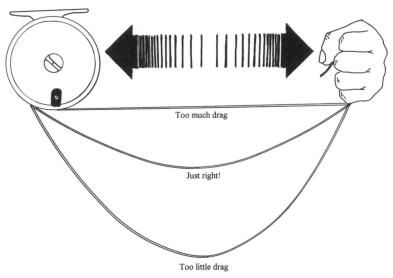

Too much drag

Just right!

Too little drag

Figure 3.8.   Drag Overrun Adjustment

little drag, increase the drag setting slowly as you pull on the reel. Alternate pulling on the reel and increasing the drag until the tippet fails, signaling that the desired drag setting has been reached.

The use of a reel with a high-quality drag, properly set, will provide ample pressure to eventually tire a fish. Still there are times when your preset reel drag alone is not enough, for example, when a fish heads for cover and you must either turn it or stop it. In most situations of this kind, the extra drag is applied manually. Reels equipped with an exposed rim, or palming rim as it is often called, afford the best opportunity to add more pressure by pressing the hand or fingers against the moving spool. This arrangement lessens the likelihood that too high a mechanical drag setting will later interfere with playing a fish as the battle unfolds. The use of rim pressure makes it possible to apply a wide range of pressure to meet changing conditions. Adding such pressure does, however, require a certain degree of dexterity and constant attention to keep from applying too much pressure at the wrong time. Also you need to keep in mind that the friction between hand and rim produces enough heat to cause a nasty burn. Caution is advised!

Manual pressure can also be applied directly to the line itself. Stu Apte, noted tarpon fisherman, wears a cotton jersey glove on his rod hand for this purpose. Tension is applied by pinching the line between the fingers or between the fingers and the handle of the rod.

Another way to increase line pressure while playing a fish would be to adjust the drag setting itself. This, however, is a dangerous practice, especially if the fish is fresh and unpredictable. Add a little too much adjustment to the drag setting and you may well lose the fish on the next long run. Sure it is less risky if the change is to lessen the drag setting, but once you change that drag you give up knowing exactly what to expect from it.

Russian roulette anyone? Unless you are very familiar with how your reel performs, determine your ideal drag setting for the conditions under which you are fishing and stick with it.

Before leaving drag systems it is important to understand that although we talk about the reel's mechanical drag function as if it were a constant, this is not the case. As each layer of line is taken off the reel, the effective or functional diameter of the reel spool becomes smaller. The functional diameter is the diameter of the reel arbor plus the added bulk created by the addition of line and backing. As you might imagine, the functional diameter varies dramatically during the course of playing a fish. This in turn affects the reel's drag. As line goes off the reel, the original drag setting remains constant but its actual drag function increases dramatically. If line is removed until the functional diameter is reduced by half, the line tension needed to engage a drag initially set at four pounds increases to eight pounds. Decrease the functional diameter to one quarter of its starting diameter, and the four-pound drag now requires sixteen pounds to engage it. To calculate the variation in drag, that is the functional drag, use the formula $FD = R1/R2 \times D$, where FD is the functional drag in pounds; $R1$ is the radius in inches of the spool when full; $R2$ is the new radius in inches; and D is the original drag setting in pounds. Understanding how drag is affected by the changes in the functional diameter of the reel will help you to understand why many fishermen are attracted to the newer large arbor reels, and why most saltwater anglers use low drag settings.

Change in the functional diameter of the reel not only affects the drag but also the speed at which the spool turns and the rate at which line is taken off or put back onto the reel. Little wonder, therefore, why reel makers and the buying public are attracted to any design change that promises a greater degree of consistency in these three variables. To look closer at how well the reel makers are doing their job, we need to focus on their most recent creation, the large arbor reel. (See figure 3.9)

First, understand that not all large arbor reels are created equal. One such reel in my collection has an arbor measuring one-and-a-half inches in diameter, double the size of that on the same reel with a standard arbor. Both reels, however, share the same reel diameter and spool width. The two spools are in fact interchangeable. This means that while the problems attributed to the wide variation of functional diameter stand to be reduced slightly, a new problem, that of insufficient reel capacity, emerges. It is only when one uses this reel with a line several sizes smaller than that suggested by the manufacturer that any significant gain is to be realized. The gain comes as the result of increasing the size of the arbor while at the same time increasing the carrying capacity of the spool, in this case by using a smaller weight line.

The best large arbor reels on the market today are not based on modifications of standard models. The best reel makers seek to provide increased overall reel diameter in keeping with a two- or threefold increase in the diameter of the arbor itself. In an effort to ensure sufficient room for backing, many of our new large arbor reels boast a wider profile. A word of caution is in order lest you jump to the conclusion that the wider the reel the better. The wider the reel the more likely it is to produce an irregular bunching up of the line on one side of the arbor or the other. Often such a bunch will collapse and trap line under itself, causing a tangle. If you have a particularly wide reel, take the time to guide the line onto the reel so it falls evenly across the entire width of the arbor.

Large arbor reels of solid design such as those sold by Bauer, Loop, Tibor, and Waterworks can improve your

ability to play a fish by providing improved drag performance and faster line retrieval with less line coiling than
standard reels. Having the ability to recover line quickly
can be an important consideration when targeting far-
ranging saltwater game fish such as albacore. Speed
demons that they are, albacore can strip a hundred yards
of line off your reel in a matter of seconds, only to make
a U-turn and head straight back at you. Oh, that terrible
feeling as you frantically try to recover all the slack and
once again bring the fish under your control.

It is a curious thing that most anglers automatically
assume that any large arbor reel will retrieve line faster
than a smaller standard size reel. Such is not always the
case. The location of the crank near the outer edge of
some large arbor requires the use of more than simple
wrist movement to turn it. Having to move the arm in
order to turn the spool can slow retrieval rate dramatically. Experiment with a variety of reels before you buy.

For those anglers looking for faster line retrieval,
you may wish to explore a type of reel known as multipliers. These reels have been around for many years but
never have found wide acceptance. Their additional
gearing, which allows up to a 3:1 retrieval rate, makes
them heavier than their conventional counterparts and
also renders their drag system less sensitive. Inciden-
tally, multipliers are not allowed in competition among
some fishing clubs.

Our discussion of reels to this point has focused on
differences in drag systems and arbor size. We now turn
the attention to drive systems, the third but not the least
important reel feature. There are two basic types of
drive systems—direct or clutch drive. On direct drive
reels, the handle mimics the rotation of the reel spool.
Turn the handle in one direction and line comes in. Turn
the handle in the opposite direction and line goes out.
Direct drive reels are tried and true, simple, reliable,

economical, and as traditional as old Izaak Walton himself. However, direct drive reels require that you let go of
the handle to allow the fish to take line when it is required to do so. This is not the case with antireverse
reels. This type of reel utilizes a special clutch and brake
system that permits the handle to mimic the rotation of
the spool only when line is being taken in. When the line
is going out, the handle remains stationary. The angler
need not worry about taking his hand off the handle and
may in fact continue reeling without fear of adding any
more line tension than his preset drag setting will allow.
It is easy to see how this feature can assist the angler
when playing a fish. Gone is the need to know precisely
when to stop reeling and when to let go of the handle to
release line tension. It also saves having to fumble
around again to find and *safely* grasp the handle once released. The word safely is emphasized here to help rein-
force the need for caution when playing any strong fish
on a direct drive reel.

Once, when playing a salmon of about twenty
pounds, I misjudged what the fish was going to do and
as a result got a debilitating rap on the knuckle of my
thumb. I thought the fish was going to hold and that it
was safe to regain my grip on the handle. However, just
as I reached for the handle the fish tore off and in doing
so set the handle in motion once more. I wasn't fast
enough to get my thumb out of the way in time to prevent the two from colliding. While freshwater fishermen are not very likely to encounter a situation like
the one described, the same cannot be said for those
fishing in saltwater where the problem occurs all too
often, sometimes, I might add, with serious injuries.
This is something for the beginning saltwater angler to
think twice about when choosing a reel.

I have heard it said in defense of using direct drive
reels that you can train anyone with a lick of sense to

keep his hands away from a moving reel handle. While this may indeed be true, the argument fails to recognize that learning to use the reels with caution slows the angler's response time. Safety issues aside, the greatest advantage of the antireverse reel is the speed with which the angler can respond.

While it is easy to see how the drag system might be used when playing a fish, it is more difficult to see how the drive system could be used for the same purpose. If you are using a direct drive reel and wish to add extra pressure on the fish, it is easy to do. All that is required is not to let go of the reel handle and keep on reeling in. Should you let go of the handle, line tension would return to that of the drag setting. To add extra pressure with an antireverse reel would require that the drag setting be increased. As mentioned earlier, increasing the drag in the midst of a battle can be risky business.

Reel designers have experimented with combining both direct and antireverse features in the same reel with some success. The late Bob McChristian of Miami, Florida, was among the first to do so with his very popular Seamaster reels. More recently, reel designer and manufacturer Karl-Heinz Henschel has come up with a radically new two drive system he calls Dual Mode (see figure 3.10). This system operates as any antireverse reel up to the point where additional line pressure is desired. Turn the handle in the direction of the retrieve and the reel operates as if it were direct drive. Let go of the handle or simply move it back slightly from the retrieving direction and the reel once again operates like an antireverse reel. The fish can take line against the preset drag. The process is repeated many times in the course of playing a fish and the drag setting remains unchanged, always there providing a comfortable margin of safety to prevent losing a fish when the unexpected occurs. A word of caution is in order, since choosing the

Figure 3.9. Large arbor reels have attracted the attention of reel designers and anglers alike. The reel pictured above is the brainchild of Karl-Heinz Henschel. Designed for saltwater use, each turn of the reel retrieves twenty inches of line.

Karl-Heinz Henschel photo.

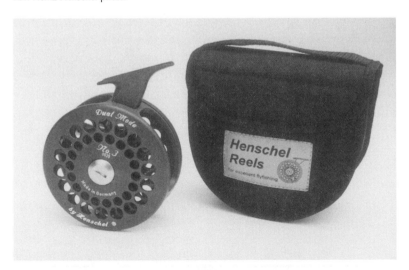

Figure 3.10. German-made Henschel reels with their patented Dual Mode feature are masterfully designed and machined.

direct drive option of the Dual Mode increases the risk of breaking a fish off to the same level inherent in direct drive reels. If you seek the maximum break off protection from your reel's mechanical drag, the antireverse is still the best choice. Whichever drive system you chose, if it is a Henschel it will be masterfully designed and manufactured. They rank among the best reels for both fresh- and saltwater use and are offered down to the lowest line weights.

Reels come in all shapes and sizes. Some offer special features to make them take in line faster, brake and operate more smoothly, and do so with greater safety. But regardless of which reel you choose, you will be confronted with the age-old question of which to chose, right or left hand wind. If you are right-hand dominant and follow the lead of spin casters and plug casters, you would reel with the secondary or left hand. This makes good sense since it uses the greater dexterity and eye/hand coordination of the dominant hand to perform the more important task of thrusting and parrying with the rod. Let the secondary left hand perform the lesser task of reeling in the line. Traditionalist and many saltwater pros would have us winding with the dominant hand. This would mean transferring the rod to the other hand after hooking a fish since casting, hooking, and reeling use the same hand. Proponents of this method say that it is worth it, arguing that the dominant hand can wind faster and longer than the secondary. Very important they say when a fish turns and runs straight for the angler. Fortunately, most of today's reels are easily converted from right to left hand wind. You decide for yourself which is best.

The reel can play an important part in fighting fish. The drag system will determine how much and how smoothly mechanical pressure is applied. The size of the arbor will impact how quickly you recover slack line. The drive system will affect how quickly and safely you can respond to changing demands for more or less line. There are many good reels on the market today. I have mentioned my favorite, Henschel, but Tibor, Billy Pate, and Islander have a large following among saltwater fishermen. Once you have decided upon the type and manufacture of reel you want, be sure to select one large enough to accommodate your fly line and backing needs. If you are planning to fish in saltwater, for example, you will need a reel that will hold an extra fifty yards of backing plus the longer 110-foot fly line. It is important that you not overfill the reel. If in doubt as to whether a reel is going to be large enough, select the next larger size. I have never regretted having done so. When properly filled, there should be an approximately one-quarter of an inch space between the line on the spool and the frame. All totaled, the reel is an important piece of fish-fighting equipment. Choose and use it wisely.

Line/Leader System

The line/leader system consists of the fly line backing, the fly line, and the leader. Should a fish make a long run, the backing provides additional length to the relatively short ninety or 110-foot fly line. The fly line serves as a flexible casting weight to aid in the presentation of the fly. The leader serves as an invisible link between the fly line and fly. When all three are in good order and working well together, they keep us attached, via the hook, to our fish. The security of this attachment rests primarily upon the strength of the leader and especially the tippet, that section of leader nearest the fly. Matching the tippet to the size and fighting characteristics of the fish species being targeted is the first of many choices the angler will be required to make with regard to the line/leader system.

I do not know of a chart that identifies proper tippet size for each species of game fish. This can be attributed to the many variables involved. The information given would have to be shown as a range of sizes so wide as to make the information of little value. What would be most useful is a system or methodology that would identify a starting point from which the angler can increase or decrease tippet size to match the equipment being used, fishing conditions, and so forth. Fortunately, such a methodology exists in the "Rule of Three."

The Rule of Three divides the size of the hook by a constant, three, to yield the tippet size in "X." If you divide twelve, the size of the hook, by three, the constant, you get four, the size of the tippet in "X" or 4X. This generally represents the heaviest or strongest tippet that would be used with your chosen size-twelve fly. (See table 3.3: Alternative Number One.)

Unfortunately, the Rule of Three works only for hook sizes one and smaller. It is, therefore, limited in its usefulness. However, another methodology yields similar recommendations using rod/line weight. Subtract one from any given rod/line weight to determine the recommended lower limit for the tippet size. Add four to the same rod/line weight to establish the upper limit. This method is based on the matched performance of rod and tippet. To go below the recommended limit increases the risk of breaking the tippet. Going above the recommended limit increases the risk of breaking the rod. When using a six weight rod, for example, five- to ten-pound test tippets are recommended. For a nine weight rod, use eight- to thirteen-pound test tippet. Although these and the other recommended tippet strengths are somewhat arbitrary, they do have general acceptance in practice and serve as a valuable starting point. (See table 3.3: Alternative Number Two.)

Table 3.3 Tippet Selection Guide

Alternative Number One: Use the Rule of Three to determine tippet diameter from hook size.
Example: 20 divided by 3 equals 6⅔ or 7X or 6X

Hook size	Tippet Size in X
20	7X or 6X
18	6X
16	5X
14	5X or 4X
12	4X
8	3X
6	2X
4	2X or 1X
2	1X or 0X
1	0X

Note: To convert tippet diameter in X to tippet strength in pounds, consult the product label on the spools of tippet you are using or use the general conversion table below.

Tippet size	7X	6X	5X	4X	3X	2X	1X	0X
Pound test	2	3	4.5	5	7	10	12	15

Alternative Number Two: Use the line weight designation for the rod to determine the range of recommended tippet size in pound test. The rod/line weight minus one is used to identify the lower recommended limit. The rod/line weight plus four is used to set the upper recommended limit. The calculations to determine the tippet size for use on a six weight rod would look like this: **6 − 1 = 5** (the lower limit) and **6 + 4 = 10** (the upper limit).

Rod/Line Weight	Pound Test Tippet
2	1–6
3	2–7
4	3–8
5	4–9
6	5–10
7	6–11
8	7–12
9	8–13
10	9–14
11	10–15
12	12–16

You may use either of the tippet selection methods described here, but keep in mind that the suggested tippets are just that, suggestions. You will need to refine your choice based on fishing conditions and your skill at playing fish. If you are ever in doubt as to which tippet to choose, it is wise to choose on the heavy side and work down. If the fish are not bothered by your heavy leader, so much the better. Using the heaviest leader possible allows you to land your fish in the shortest time possible.

Playing a fish on very light tippets, those two or three "X" sizes below what would be considered customary, requires careful attention to what the fish you are playing is doing. A sudden jerk on a tight leader can easily break the tippet. While a two-pound overload represents a modest 20 percent increase when ten-pound tippet is being used, it represents a whopping 66+ percent overload when three-pound tippet is being used. Clearly, the use of lighter than normal tippets can mean a lot of fish being broken off or played to exhaustion for fear of breaking them off. Fortunately, there are ways to close the gap between the ability to bring a fish to net quickly and the use of light tippets. The first of these ways has already been mentioned, namely, the use of a long, soft action rod that acts to reduce the violent nature of a sudden jerk through increased shock absorbency. The noodle rod represents the extreme of this practice.

The second way to increase one's chances of landing fish on a light tippet is to increase the shock absorbency of the leader itself. This can be done simply by increasing the length of the tippet, which serves to allow for more stretch. The use of an elastic material, power gum, in the butt of the leader carries the idea of a shock absorbing leader one step further to create what some call a bungee butt.

A third alternative focuses on honing one's fish-fighting skills, especially that of being better able to anticipate the fish's next move. Knowing the fighting characteristics of the fish you are playing will contribute greatly to your success. So important is this knowledge that a chapter on the subject is included later in this book.

Once you have determined the size of the tippet you are going to use, you can focus your attention on which material and knots to use in the construction and later in the attachment of the leader to the fly line. Nylon monofilament and fluorocarbon are the most common leader materials in use today. They both offer high degrees of strength to diameter, resistance to abrasion, stretch, and knot strength. Unfortunately what is offered is not equal. There are times when we are forced to choose one over the other. Nylon, for example, offers a better strength to diameter ratio than fluorocarbon, but the latter offers slightly better resistance to abrasion. Nylon becomes brittle and weakens when exposed to the sun; fluorocarbon is impervious to ultraviolet rays. Nylon absorbs water, which acts to reduce its breaking strength slightly when saturated after long submersion; fluorocarbon does not absorb water. Hence, the wet and dry breaking strength is the same.

It must be noted, however, that the differences in the performance of these two materials is not so great under normal fishing conditions as to make one or the other stand out as the better choice. Preference is usually a matter of individual experience, tradition, or isolated fishing situation such as trying to horse sheepshead from around bridge pylons, in which case the better resistance to abrasion would make fluorocarbon the better choice. Do a little experimenting on your own so as to become better acquainted with these two materials and the effect each has upon the fishing you do. The final choice is yours to make.

Some caution is advised when purchasing leader material. Monofilament, for example, degrades under long exposure to heat and ultraviolet rays. Improper storage or handling can render even the most recently stocked merchandise useless, reducing breaking and knot strength by as much as half. Always test the leader material you plan to purchase. The shop owner may have a preference as to whether you test before or after the purchase, but do test before you leave the shop. The easiest test to perform, the stretch test, is based upon the knowledge that monofilament that has been exposed to heat and/or ultraviolet rays loses its ability to stretch. The test, therefore, is to wrap some of the leader material around each hand and stretch it between them by pulling the hands apart. Take note of the amount of stretch present and how much force is required to break the material. If the line breaks easier than expected or seems to lack stretch, return it and try another spool or go elsewhere to make your purchase. Leader material left in your fishing vest from one year to the next also needs to be tested before use. If you happen to be fishing when you do the test and discover that your leader is rotten, try spooling several feet of material off the spool and repeating the stretch test. Material buried underneath a protective layer of several wraps is often less damaged. This simple procedure can often save the day.

Another word of caution when selecting leader materials is of particular concern for those seeking to have their catch included in IGFA (International Game Fish Association) record books. Some manufacturers of leader materials make it a practice to slightly understate the breaking strength of their products. It is a bit of marketing psychology I guess; better to have the consumer get more than expected than less. However, when a tippet labeled three-pound tippet proves upon an official weigh-in to be four pounds and as a result the catch is disqualified, someone is going to be very disappointed. The use of IGFA-class leader material will prevent this from happening to you, but if you ever find yourself wondering what the actual breaking strength of your leader material really is, let me suggest this simple procedure.

Begin with a length of leader secured at one end to a hook and the other to the handle of a bucket. With the bucket suspended only an inch or two above the floor or a tabletop, begin filling the bucket with dry sand and continue to do so until the line breaks. Examine the line to determine that the break did in fact occur in the line itself and not at the knot due to knot failure. If knot failure was the cause, repeat the procedure using stronger knots. The Bimini Twist, for example, allows a double-line connection to the hook or pail handle. When it has been determined that the break occurred in the line, the only thing left to do in order to determine the breaking strength of the line is to weigh the bucket of sand. The most accurate scale that would be readily available is probably the one at your local supermarket. State laws require scales used in commerce to undergo regular testing and certification.

Knot strength obviously plays a significant part in line/leader performance and should always be considered a suspect of any line/leader failure. Make it a practice anytime you break a fish off to examine the break to determine the cause. If the break is clean, almost as if cut with a knife, the break was the result of line failure. In other words, the breaking strength of the line was exceeded. If, on the other hand, the break reveals a sharp bend or curl, the failure can be attributed to knot failure. Wind knots, those nasty little overhand knots that get into your leader as the result of bad casting, can, if not detected and removed, reduce line strength by as much as half. They are of special interest here because breaks caused by wind knots often present themselves as if cut by a knife, lacking the bend or curl of typical knot failure. The evidence they leave behind can be misleading. Make it a habit to inspect your leader periodically and always after making a bad cast in order to detect wind knots and remove them before they tighten and become a problem. Knots are key to the integrity of the line/leader system because they are the weakest link and as such require our careful attention.

Knot failure can be attributed to two basic causes. The first is the use of a knot for a purpose other than the one for which it was intended. The second is the use of a knot that has been improperly tied. Knots used in the line/leader system are called upon to perform four major tasks: join backing to the reel arbor, backing to the fly line, fly line to the leader, and leader to the hook. No one knot can be expected to perform all these tasks with equal strength and reliability so we must select the right knot for each job.

Among the contenders for best knot to use when joining backing to the reel arbor are the Arbor knot and the Duncan Loop or uni-knot. Although the Arbor knot is most often used, I prefer the uni-knot because it has better shock strength. If you have ever had a fish take all your line and backing off the reel, then you know that shock strength is the only thing you have going for you when the line comes tight against the knot. But how often does this situation occur? The arbor knot on the other hand is easier to tie, although neither is difficult. Choose either one. If you use gel-spun lines such as Fusion, Spiderwire, Spectron, or Orvis's Gel-Spun in place of more traditional dacron backing, use the uni-knot, increasing the number of wraps used in its construction from five to eight. Some saltwater anglers form a Bimini Twist at the reel end of the gel-spun backing then use the uni-knot to attach the double line to the reel spool.

The knot joining the backing to the reel is seldom tested in use. However, the knot used to attach backing to the fly line my be tested several times during the season, especially if you are fishing salt water. You will want to look for a strong knot that flows smoothly through the guides. The Nail knot is the first choice among freshwater anglers because it is easy to tie and presents a slim profile that passes through the guides easily. However, it has been known to fail under more extreme saltwater conditions such as when fighting large tarpon. Angling illustrator and fly tier Fishy Fullum is a self-proclaimed connector maniac. If he loses a fish because of knot failure his whole day is ruined. After experiencing several bad days due to knot failure at the fly line to leader connection, Fishy and some of his fishing buddies began using a knot that appears to be a modification of the Key West knot. He recommends it highly and suggests that I pass it along to you.

The tying procedure begins by tying a loose overhand knot at the tag end of the fly line. The tag end of the backing is passed through the center of this knot and the overhand knot is tightened to hold it securely. A "trombone" loop is formed in the backing so as to lay alongside the fly line's standing part. The tag end of the backing is wrapped around and then through the trombone loop. The knot in the backing is brought up snug against the overhand knot in the fly line and tightened. The tag end of the fly line is trimmed on a diagonal and covered with a whip finish to complete the knot. (See figure 3.11.)

The use of either the Nail knot or Fishy's knot fails to meet the special needs of those who change fly lines often. A better choice for these anglers is to use a loop-to-loop connection. The extra time it takes to prepare

Figure 3.11.   Fishy's Knot

the two interconnecting loops is returned in full measure each time the line is changed.

A loop-to-loop connection between backing and fly line requires a loop in the backing and one in the fly line. Since the backing and fly line are made of different materials, their loops will not be constructed in the same way. When forming loops in the backing, the Surgeon's Loop, a variation of the Surgeon's knot or the Perfection loop are most popular. For those seeking an even stronger loop, follow the lead of many saltwater anglers who use a Bimini Twist loop that is large enough to allow the reel to be passed through it. This loop is more reliable when gel-spun type backings are being used. Nevertheless, the slim profile, strength, and all-around good looks of the Splice Loop make it the top choice whenever the backing is braided to produce a hollow core. Although a splicing tool is required to make the loop, it is easy to make and use. The tool consists of a twelve-inch piece of fine stainless steel wire measuring about .010 of an inch in diameter that has been sharply bent in the middle of its length to produce a "V" shape.

The Splice Loop is made by inserting the point of the splicing tool into the hollow center of the braided backing at a point four inches longer than twice the length of the desired loop. The tool is advanced two-and-one-half inches in the direction of the tag end where it is made to exit. The tag end is doubled back over itself and the very tip inserted between the two legs of the splicing tool. The tool is withdrawn, carrying with it the tag end of the line itself. When the tag end emerges at the place where the tool was originally inserted, an inch-and-one-half length of line is extracted. The tool is once again inserted into the center of the line, but this time at a point two inches away from where the first insertion took place. Once inserted into the hollow center, the tool is advanced one and one-half inch, exiting the line one-half inch short of the point where the

tag from the first procedure exited. The tag is again inserted into the splicing tool and the loop is withdrawn, carrying with it the tag end of the line. Because the length of
the tag is shorter than the length of the distance traveled
by the splicing tool, the tag is lost inside the hollow braid.
A drop of super glue applied to the line at the point where
the tag now lies hidden completes the splice loop. For an
illustration of the completed loop, see figure 3.12.

Unlike loops in backing, a loop formed by doubling
the fly line may be too bulky to clear the guides
smoothly. Most light line, freshwater anglers, therefore,
prefer loop connectors made of braided nylon. These
loop connectors that resemble the Splice Loop are readily available at most fly shops. If you find that you need
help installing them, check the shop where you bought
them. Chances are they will do the job for you. For the
do-it-yourselfer, loops can be prefabricated at home using
twenty- to twenty-five-pound nylon braid. A hundred-
yard spool makes a bazillion loops. Connecting loops are
attached to the fly line using super glue. To help prevent
the cut edge of the loop from fraying with use, a small
piece of elastic tubing is used to cover the rear end of the
splice. As an added security measure, a whip finish can
be substituted for the elastic tubing.

The popularity of the Braided Loop is best attributed to its slim profile and its ease in passing through the
guides rather than its strength, which I have found ques-
tionable at times. When strength alone is the determining factor, a better choice is a loop formed from the fly
line itself. The first and best that comes to mind in this
category is the Double Nail knot loop, a loop formed in
the fly line and held securely in place by two Nail knots
tied using eight- to ten-pound mono. (See figure 3.13.)

The Nail knot or the connecting loops used to join
the backing to the fly line can also be used to connect the
leader to the fly line. The result, however, is not nearly as

glue

Figure 3.12. The Splice Loop

long lasting. The stiffness of the nylon leader and the constant flexing of line as it is being cast combine to limit the life of the connection to a dozen or so long days on the water. Damage usually presents itself as a crack in the coating of the fly line, usually at the base of the knot or loop. Undetected, the crack widens to eventually expose the core of the fly line, which frays easily with continued use, weakening the line and diminishing both strength and casting performance. Although the Nail knot yields a connection with a shorter lifespan than that of connecting loops, its more compact and rigid connection offers better casting performance. Again, another choice to make. You must decide which method, knot or loops, best meets your needs. However, if you choose to use interlocking loops to make the connection, caution is in order. Improperly done, connecting two loops can result in a weak girth hitch rather than the stronger and more desirable interlock that resembles a Square knot. (See figure 3.14.)

Selecting which knots to use when building or repairing leaders also requires making choices. The choices, however, are less a matter of personal preference and more an attempt to meet a need dictated by one of the many different situations one is likely to encounter. The most common situation involves joining lengths of monofilament to build or repair a leader or its tippet, the last and finest section. The Surgeon's knot or the Blood knot are the knots of choice to perform this important function. Most anglers choose one to the exclusion of the other. The more knowledgeable angler uses both, choosing one over the other as the situation dictates. If, for example, the lines to be joined are of dissimilar diameter, greater than .002 of an inch or 2X, or the knot needs to be tied quickly or under fading light conditions, the Surgeon's knot is used. Use the Blood knot for joining fine tippet material, 5X and below, or for

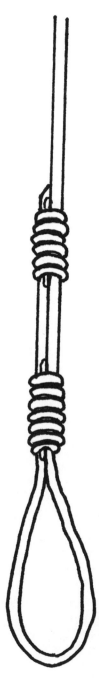

Figure 3.13.   The Double Nail Knot Loop

RIGHT - Square knot

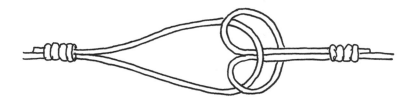

WRONG - Girth hitch

Figure 3.14.   Loop to Loop Connections

joining two sections of line when only the tag ends are free, such as when repairing a break in the leader with a fly still attached to the tippet section. When grass or algae in the water makes keeping the leader clean a problem, avoid using the Surgeon's knot because of its bulk. The Blood knot is less likely to collect debris.

Not all monofilament leader material is the same. Some are harder or less resistant to abrasion than others. Their individual characteristics may be at odds with one another so as to weaken the final product. For this reason it is best to use the same brand of material for all construction and repairs to your leader. Monofilament and fluorocarbon materials should never be mixed for the same reason as above.

A special situation exists for saltwater fishermen and those freshwater anglers who target pike and musky because of their need to attach a large diameter shock leader or bite guard to their light leaders. The Albright knot is an excellent choice for the job. Heavy shock leaders that may be five or more times the diameter of the leader to which it is to be attached can be joined using this knot. The Bimini Twist with a Huffnagle knot, the choice of offshore fishermen, serves the same purpose, but features a Double Line loop in the finer diameter leader. This serves to substantially increase the strength of the connection and to allow the use of a very heavy shock leader of the eighty- to one-hundred-pound class. Although beyond the range of most fly fishermen, the use of bite guards made of wire may at times be required such as when fishing for sharks and barracuda. When single strand wire is used for the bite guard, a Haywire Twist loop is made in wire and then flattened to form an elongated loop. A Bimini Twist is tied in the mono leader and the double line is thus created for use to connect the mono leader to the wire loop using an Albright knot. When braided wire is used instead of the single strand, the Haywire Twist loop is not needed. The wire to mono leader connection is directly made using the same doubled line of the Bimini Twist as described above for tying an Albright knot. While use of wire as part of leader construction is pretty far afield for the majority of fishermen, the use of elastic material such as paragum, power gum, or bungee butt to build super shock absorbing leaders goes even further afield.

The use of elastic leader material is an innovative attempt at catching large fish, usually trout, using the finest of tippet material and the smallest of flies. The system itself consists of a section of elastic leader tied in between sections of mono leader usually just before the final tippet section. The special characteristics of the material requires use of one of two specialized knots, either the Para Gum knot or the Vice Versa knot. The former, a pair of uniknots tied back to back. The latter, a knot new to me, was developed by Harry Asher and described by Geoffrey Budworth in his book *The Complete Book of Fishing Knots.*

The knots used in connecting sections of line or leader to one another are many and varied to meet the demands imposed by material or circumstance. The knots used to connect the leader to the hook are even greater in number and diversity. My own research has produced a list of some twenty knots, a lot of conflicting test results, and no small degree of frustration. Here are the six knots I have found to be the best for making this all-important connection.

When using very light tippets with the smallest of hooks, use the improved Clinch knot. If the tippet being used is fine enough to pass through the eye of the hook twice, but no larger than 0X or .011 inches in diameter, use either the Trilene knot or the Jansik special. The Trilene knot is a modification of the clinch knot and is well-known among anglers. The Jansik special is relatively unknown, but so impressed me during my own research that I have begun using it. Both of these knots offer the added security of a double loop through the eye. For more information see *The Complete Book of Fishing Knots* written by Geoffrey Budworth.

The use of heavy tippets, those generally exceeding fifteen-pound test, require different knots than those recommended above. Because of their inherent stiffness, it is hard to get the knot to tighten properly. In his book *Practical Fishing Knots*, which he coauthored with Mark Sosin, Lefty Kreh recommends using the non-slip loop as the knot of choice for the job. He cautions, however, that the number of turns of the tag end around the standing part is reduced as the test of the line increases. For example, use five turns for eight- to twelve-pound test, four for fifteen- to forty-pound, and three for fifty- to sixty-pound test. Use the Haywire Twist for connecting the hook to single-strand wire. The old tried-and-true Figure 8 knot is best when braided rather than when single wire is being used.

Table 3.4 provides a list of recommended knots. Their selection is the result of personal experience and investigation. Some knots that showed real promise in the literature were simply too difficult to tie easily and would prove even more so under actual fishing conditions. If you are dissatisfied with the performance of the knots you are now using or simply curious about the recommended alternatives, let me encourage you to do a little exploring on you own. Use the knot books cited in the bibliography as a starting point. I think you will enjoy the trip.

Before closing the discussion on lines and leaders, two conservation-related issues deserve consideration. Any discarded leader material left lying around in the water or on the riverbank has the potential to entrap small animals and birds. Properly disposing of leader materials has always been a concern of the conservation-minded, but the

Table 3.4.   Recommended Knots for the Line/Leader System

Backing to Reel Arbor	Arbor Knot
	Duncan Loop (Uni-knot)
Backing to Fly Line	Nail Knot
	Surgeon's Loop (backing)
	Perfection Loop (backing)
	Splice Loop (backing)
	Braided Nylon Loop (fly line)
	Double Nail Knot Loop (fly line)
Fly Line to Leader	Nail Knot
	Braided Nylon Loop (fly line)
	Double Nail Knot Loop (fly line)
	Surgeon's Loop (leader)
	Perfection Loop (leader)
Leader Sections to One Another	Surgeon's Loop
	Blood Knot
Leader to Heavy Shock Tippet	Albright Knot
	Bimini Twist with Huffnagle Knot
Leader to Bungee	Para Gum Knot
	Vice Versa Knot
Leader to Hook	Improved Clinch
	Trilene Knot
	Jansik Special
	Non-slip Loop (for heavy mono tippets)
	Haywire Twist (for single wire)
	Figure-8 Knot (for braided wire)

fact that the monofilament is biodegradable serves to reduce its threat to wildlife. Fluorocarbon, on the other
hand, is not biodegradable. Those who choose to use it
must be mindful of its lethality and take extra measures to
see that waste material is disposed of properly.

The second issue arose quite unexpectedly one day
while talking about the strength of various knots used to
tie the leader to the hook. When I told a friend that I had

found a new knot that was stronger than the breaking strength of the line, he said he would not use such a knot to attach his fly to his leader. He went on to explain that he wanted the weakest link in his line/leader system to be at the hook so in case the line should break, the break would occur at the hook, not several inches or even feet up the leader. The thought of a fish swimming around with a length of leader trailing behind it was unacceptable. He feared that it could tangle causing injury or death. His point is noted for your consideration.

This chapter has been about choices, particularly those made in the selection of the equipment we choose to fish with. Of all the misconceptions about the playing fish, the most damaging is the belief that the process of playing a fish begins the moment it is hooked. Quite the contrary, for as we have seen in this chapter, choosing the right equipment plays a major role in fish-playing success. But what is true of equipment selection can also be said of the conditions under which the fishing takes place. Having a carefully thought-out battle plan will pay big dividends once the fish is hooked and the fight begins. The next chapter explores common fishing conditions, their hazards, and how best to deal with them.

FOUR

BEYOND THE RULES— FISHING CONDITIONS

As we have seen from the foregoing chapter, the angler's success with landing the biggest fish of his life begins long before the fish is hooked. This holds true for the selection of equipment prior to the trip, as well as for the selection of conditions under which we choose to fish. If fishing in saltwater from a boat, for example, your fish-playing tactics would be somewhat different than if you were wade fishing in a fast flowing river. This chapter explores some of the unique problems that are frequently encountered under common fishing conditions and suggests ways to deal with them. If you are new to this sport or making the transition from still to moving water, from fresh to saltwater, or from wading to being in a boat, you will find this information of particular value.

Moving Water and Still Water

The force of the water is itself the prime concern of those who fish in moving water. It can be made to work both for or against the angler. Whenever an angler is in a position downstream or below the fish being played, he has the clear advantage. The fish carries the full burden of the water against its body, the force of the water against the line and leader, and any additional line pressure that the angler might apply. This combination of forces can quickly tire the strongest fish and for this reason a fish will not tolerate it for long. The angler must be ready to counter the fish's attempts to change position. If a fish is successful in getting downstream of the angler, it would gain the advantage formerly enjoyed by him.

It is very difficult for the downstream angler to stop a fish from turning and heading toward him. Fish can turn on a dime and the angler is in no position to exert any counter pressure to stop the maneuver. However, after the turn is made, the angler is in a position to limit the fish's run and perhaps even keep the fish from getting downstream of his position. Side pressure is applied so as to make the fish work hard if it is to stay on its downstream course. This extra work speeds the rate that oxygen is used and shortens the time that passes before the fish once again turns to face upstream, a position in which it can respire more easily. The ability of the angler to quickly take in the slack that results as the fish moves downstream, toward an angler, is important. The desired side pressure cannot be applied until the slack is removed and the line brought under tension. Fast retrieval of line also works to keep the distance between fish and angler short. This affords the angler a greater degree of leverage and, in turn, greater control. If all the angler's efforts to keep the fish upstream fail, there is not a moment to lose.

Once the fish gets below an angler the odds are that the fish will be lost.

It is almost impossible to bring a big fish to net if it requires dragging it upstream through heavy flow. The weight of the fish combined with the force of the water against it and against the line and leader generate higher than normal line tension. A quick turn or bolt in any direction except upstream would be enough to break an already strained tippet. Assuming that the angler is not able to get into a position downstream of the fish, side pressure can be used to force the fish to move rather than just holding stationary, tethered there by the line and resting. Applying side pressure can also be successful in moving the fish out of the main flow into calmer water along the edges of the flow. If the side pressure fails to bring about desired results, try some of the strategies discussed in chapter 1. You might, for example, feed out slack line and allow it to belly well downstream of the fish. This maneuver creates pressure from below the fish and often triggers its natural response to move in a direction opposite the one restraining it. I still sense the amazement I felt the first time I tried this. I stood bug-eyed at the tail of a pool, watching as the fish and my bright orange fly line headed upstream. Although the force of moving water is most often seen as a negative, it can be made to work on the angler's behalf.

Boats and Wading

Whether fishing in moving water or still, those who fish from a boat enjoy the advantage of being able to position themselves to greater advantage when fighting fish. They can, for example, pursue a fleeing fish and keep it at hand where it can be fought more effectively. Tired of losing stripers to the rocks when fishing close to shore,

Gardner Grant, a well-known fisherman, uses his boat to "walk" stripers away from the rocky shore to deeper water much as one would walk a trout upstream.

The advantages attributed to fishing from a boat generally assume that more than one person is involved. In such cases boat operator and angler must work as a team. It is the responsibility of the angler to let the boat operator know what he desires. Perhaps it is to get closer to the fish, to back away, or to position the boat on one side or the other. The responsibility of the boat operator, on the other hand, goes beyond meeting the needs of the angler with regard to positioning the boat to include the angler's safety as well. Any sudden move or turn could throw the preoccupied angler off balance and cause a serious injury. Hence, the two-way communication between boat operator and angler is essential. Watch two boat anglers who have been fishing together for a long time play and land a fish. Their high degree of cooperation makes it easy to understand why boat anglers use "we" when talking about the fish that were caught on their trip.

The ability to maneuver into the most advantageous position from which to fight a fish is the boat fisherman's greatest advantage over his wading counterpart. However, all the things that project from the boat or hang in the water from its sides or bottom can cause a line to tangle and a fish to be lost. Motors, oars, oarlocks, anchors, dangling legs, coolers, gear bags, and anything else that might catch on the line is an object to be reckoned with. If it cannot be removed as a threat, a plan needs to be devised as to how you might deal with a tangle should it occur. In most situations, giving slack to calm a fish would allow you the time needed to remedy whatever problem you may be having. However, your primary efforts should focus on prevention.

Those fishing from a boat are frequently faced with having a fish go under it and pass to the other side. To counter this move, the angler puts the tip of the rod deep into the water to keep the line from tangling around the propeller and walks the rod tip around to the same side the fish is on. At the first sign of any trouble, give slack until the line has been cleared, then resume the fight. If the fish goes deep and holds, the situation becomes more serious.

Any fish that is holding is a resting fish. The angler can ill afford to let the situation exist for any length of time. The wading fisherman uses maximum pressure applied to the side to get the fish moving. Positioned directly above the holding fish, the boat angler lacks the same leverage so he must resort to brute strength to bring the fish off the bottom and get it moving. The technique of pumping the rod is the most effective way of applying the needed pressure for the job at hand.

To pump the rod means to slowly raise the rod tip from just off the surface of the water to about forehead level or forty-five degrees from the water while keeping the line tight. The rod tip is then lowered quickly, but smoothly, as the line, now under less tension, is reeled in. The same maneuver is repeated over and over until the fish, which is slowly being raised to the surface, abandons its efforts to stay near the bottom in favor of flight or fight. Pumping is a technique that every boat fisherman needs to know and is one that is especially important to those who target big freshwater fish such as pike or musky or saltwater fish such as tarpon. Should pumping prove ineffective, try moving the boat one to two hundred yards off to the side of where the fish is holding and again apply the pressure. This technique reduces the angle of rise and, even more important, changes the pressure from top to side.

The growing popularity of personal fishing crafts (PFCs), such as float tubes, kick boats, and pontoon boats, creates some interesting and challenging fish-fighting situations. If the angler/operator wishes to change his position when playing a fish, must he put the rod down in order to do so?

Most users of PFCs give little consideration to how their choice might affect their ability to play fish. Matters regarding convenience and personal comfort seem to take preference. Pontoon boats are highly rated because of the degree of comfort, safety, and mobility afforded the user even in swift flowing rivers. Their use as a fish-fighting platform, however, is severely limited by the fact that primary locomotion and control requires the use of oars. Unless you are particularly adept at fighting a fish with the rod in one hand and operating the boat with oars in the other, you would find fighting fish from a pontoon craft a poor option. It would be best to beach the craft and wade while fishing.

While the use of more traditional type float tubes are not recommended in moving water, they do afford the stillwater anglers the ability to control their crafts without sacrificing their ability to fight a fish. The use of specially designed foot fins facilitates hands-free operation. The same advantage can be enjoyed by those who use kick boat type PFCs. While oars are provided on this type of craft, they are best used for control and locomotion. Their safe use in moving water serves to separate kick boats from float tubes as the better choice of fishing craft. They also make better fishing platforms than the safer and more comfortable pontoon crafts, which are best used for transportation to and from fishing locations. PFCs provide the lone angler with many of the benefits enjoyed for years by those who fished from boats. However, they best serve the angler's fish-fighting needs when they provide a means of hands-free maneuverability and control.

Most of the time when I think of wading, I think of rivers and streams. There are, however, a growing number of anglers who do their wading on flats and along beaches. Fish in shallow water are as spooky as they come; their blistering dash for safety can create a problem for the angler. A low rod tip is recommended unless there are obstacles to be avoided, in which case, the often seen rod-held-high-above-the-head position is in order. A word of caution: this position puts additional strain on the tippet, and the risk of a break off is increased.

Anglers who fish from beaches are faced with having to deal with strong waves and rips. While an incoming wave can lift and push a fish toward the shore, the same fish, if caught in the backwash, can be carried back out to sea. It is important to keep line pressure constant and smoothly applied while adjusting to the push and pull of the waves. Apply a little extra pressure as the wave lifts the fish; this can be done by moving back up the beach. Slack off pressure slightly as the wave recedes. If you are going to beach your fish, take full advantage of the lifting action of the incoming waves to draw the fish high onto the beach.

Rips running along the shoreline pose still another problem for those who wade the beaches. Fish will use the fast flowing water in much the same way as a fish in a river uses a heavy current as an escape route to safety. The fisherman's best response where possible is to follow the fish, keeping the distance between them as short as possible and applying side pressure to eventually move the fish out of the rip and into calmer waters.

Saltwater and Fresh Water

The saltwater environment is corrosive, the fish large, strong, and for the most part fast. Saltwater equipment must be robust. Reels are large, heavily anodized or constructed of noncorrosive metals. Their drags are designed and constructed to withstand the high heat build up that accompanies long, high-speed runs and to do this without fading. Saltwater fly rods also differ from their freshwater counterparts in their design. They feature a heavier butt section, with or without a fighting mid-grip, and oversized guides. Saltwater lines and leader systems are strong, abrasion resistant, and scaled to match the big fish they are designed to subdue. Because of their size, speed, and endurance, saltwater fish challenge not only the angler's equipment, but his physical endurance, line managing, and fish-fighting skills as well.

Saltwater fish are fast. Their prime means of escape in their open seas environment is to outswim or outleap their pursuers. The saltwater angler must therefore be prepared to deal with reel-screaming runs. The first few seconds after a fish has been hooked are the most important. Any slack line that has been allowed to fall to the deck as the fly was being retrieved must now be carefully and quickly managed or it will become tangled as the fish streaks away. There is real danger here of injury to the angler if the line becomes tangled around fingers or hand. Two line handling techniques are helpful in this regard.

To keep accumulated slack line from getting tangled as it is being taken out by the fish, the angler forms an "O" or a tube around the line using the thumb and fingers of the line hand that he then uses to direct the line out of harm's way. Keeping the line hand directly above the line on the deck, rather than to the side, reduces the likelihood of it tangling. (See figure 4.2.) Special attention needs to be given to keeping the line from catching underfoot, on loose clothing, or around the reel. I mention these three potential problems in particular because they are the most common. However, getting line

Figure 4.1. Captain Paul Dixon of East Hampton, New York, hooks a tarpon in the Florida Keys. The first few seconds after a fish has been hooked are the most important. Any slack line that has been allowed to fall to the deck as the fly was retrieved must now be carefully and quickly managed lest it become tangled as the fish streaks away.

Gordy Hill Photo

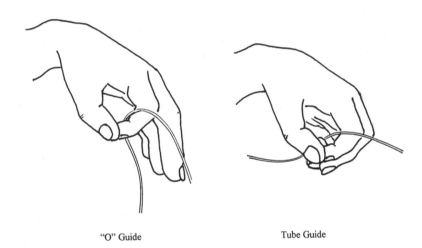

"O" Guide   Tube Guide

Figure 4.2.   Two Slack-Line Guides

caught around the reel is the one that I am bound never to forget. I learned a valuable lesson on the day I hooked into my first albacore.

I was fishing with friends Joan Wulff and George Simon off Montauk Point, Long Island, one beautiful November day when we ran into several schools of albacore. They were feeding on baitfish near the surface and the action was hot and heavy. Joan and George had each hooked and landed fish so all the attention was on me. It was my turn on the bow. Although I could get the fish to follow by fly all the way to the boat, I wasn't having much success at a hook up. As time passed and my level of frustration increased, I became obsessed with the task and devoted my full attention on trying to hook one. When at last a fish took my fly, I was so relieved that I breathed a big sigh and followed it with a shout of excitement. My time would have been better used clearing the line, which went zinging through the guides. I did not notice the loop of line that had wrapped itself around the reel until it was too late to do anything about it. The line tightened around the reel, broke, and the fish was gone. Also gone was my chance to land my first albacore. Fortunately, other than for my slightly bruised ego, my failure to manage the slack line did not result in an injury.

In most cases saltwater fishermen are spared the trouble of having to wind slack onto the reel. Hook into a fish and in seconds both it and the slack have disappeared. Sometimes, however, a hooked fish may hesitate and afford the angler the opportunity to hold it long enough for any slack line to be wound onto the reel before the fish panics and runs off. The technique is referred to as "getting a fish onto the reel." The angler controls the fish and holds it steady with line tension while at the same time reeling in any slack. This technique involves two steps, although both are preformed simultaneously.

The first step is to keep the line tight and control the fish. This is achieved by passing the line under the first or second finger of the rod hand and pressing the line against the cork grip while applying pressure with the rod. The second step is to apply tension to the line being wound onto the reel as the slack is being taken up. Failure to do this may cause the line to bunch up on the reel and cause a tangle later as the line comes off. The required tension is achieved by passing the line under the little finger of the rod hand and pressing the line against the grip. (See figure 4.3.) The need to apply varying degrees of tension at two different places while reeling in line complicates the seemingly simple procedure. It is best to practice this technique before using it on heavy fish. You will need some time to learn ways to keep your fingers from getting caught as the line becomes tight between fish and reel.

Managing line is more than getting the fish on the reel. It also includes keeping track of slack line so as not to step on it or get it tangled while lying on the deck. Saltwater anglers in Florida joke that the most famous fly line is one called "sneaker-seeker." You know, the one that always gets under your sneaker and causes you to lose a fish. To keep from standing on my line when fishing in warm climates, I remove my sneakers and fish in my stocking feet. If it is too cold to do this comfortably, as when fishing albees in the fall, I rely on a stripping basket. A new twist on the stripping basket is a wastebasket-shaped cylinder that rests on the deck and into which slack line is placed. The device is called a Fly Line Tamer and is manufactured by a firm called Pro-Trim in Islamorada, Florida.

The tremendous strength and speed of many saltwater game fish dictates careful line management. This same strength and speed can also test the angler's endurance. Learning to tire these big fish is another essential part of fishing in saltwater.

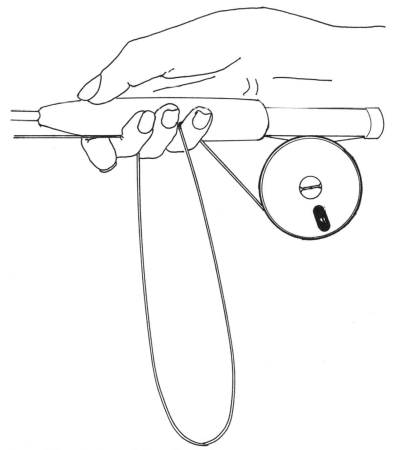

Figure 4.3.   Getting a Fish on the Reel

Saltwater experts are unanimous in their belief that the closer the fish is to the angler, the greater the effectiveness of any pressure applied. There are, however, several techniques for doing so. Stu Apte, a world-famous tarpon angler, attributes his ability to boat a hundred-pound-plus tarpon on ten-pound tippet in under twenty minutes to two techniques. One of his techniques he refers to as "getting the angle." The other he calls "down and dirty."

The angle Stu Apte seeks to establish and maintain is formed by positioning his line along the fish's side and running parallel to it. The angle between the side of the fish and the line is very narrow. The direction of the pull is to the rear, as if to pull the fish backward. If the fish attempts to turn, pressure is applied in the direction opposite the turn.

Stu Apte's "down and dirty" technique starts with the above angle then positions the tip of the rod low in the water while keeping the butt high. More often than not the rod will invert, which is conforming to its natural bend, just doing so upside down. Anytime the fish falters in its attempt to escape, extra pressure is applied down and to the side in an effort to roll the fish onto its side, causing it to become disoriented and to lose its will to fight. Although this technique was designed for fighting tarpon, it can be used to fight other large surface fighting fish in both fresh and saltwater. I have seen a similar technique used to stop running steelhead. However, in this case the rod tip is placed underwater as far below the level of the fish as practical and the pressure is smoothly applied over some distance.

The two techniques discussed above are designed to tire a fish and bring the fight to a speedy conclusion. When the objective is more immediate and designed to turn a fish in order to gain control, pressure is best applied from the side opposite where the fish wants to go

Figure 4.4. Good friend, Gordy Hill, doing the "down and dirty" to bring the pressure to bear on a tarpon he is playing.

Gordy Hill Photo

and at an angle approaching ninety degrees. However, the use of any of these techniques must give consideration to the risk of a break off, which each possesses. The assessment of the risk must take into account two factors—the speed and direction of the forces at play. The shock to the line caused by a fish bolting forward to counter the pull of the line from behind is, for example, slower but of longer duration than the same fish shocking the line as it jerks sideways in response to pressure from the side.

Choosing one kind of shock over the other is a choice between the lesser of two evils. Better the angler decides the question by the way he plays the fish than to let the fish decide based on its natural escape responses. If the angler is positioned to play a fish from behind with the line held along its side, he can expect the fish to bolt at any time and when it does, travel for a considerable distance. When the fish does bolt, the angler points the tip of his rod at the fish until the fish stops running. If, on the other hand, the angler is positioned to play a fish from the side, with the line pulling at a right angle to the side of the fish, the angler should not be surprised when it jerks its head violently to the side opposite the source of the pressure. Although of short duration, this shock is far more violent. The ninety-degree hold as described in chapter 1 affords some protection by allowing for maximum shock absorbency through the rod.

The efficient use of pressure to tire a fish quickly is the key to successful fishing everywhere but takes on special meaning when fishing in saltwater. The strength and endurance of both fish and fisherman, and everything he might know about fighting fish, will be tested to the max. Therefore, I highly recommend to anyone just getting started in saltwater fishing that they get themselves booked with a good guide to help

teach them the ropes. I can think of no better invest-
ment for the money.

Snags and Obstructions

Impediments to fighting fish take two major forms—
snags and obstructions. Snags are things such as the remains of fallen trees, rock outcroppings, coral heads, or
oyster beds. They are usually naturally occurring and
characteristically go undetected until they are discovered quite by accident in the course of playing a fish. By
this time it is too late to avoid them; react we must. With
few exceptions the best reaction is to give slack and wait
for the fish to make a change in direction that might afford us an opportunity to steer it away or free it from the
snag. If it appears that the fish's movements are restricted, try changing your position to get a better angle
or move closer to the snag in hopes of freeing the line.
In the video *The Fly Fishermen's World*, Lee Wulff is
shown passing his rod through a snag of tangled brush in
order to free his line and continue the fight in the open
water that lies on the other side.

Obstructions, the second form of impediment, are
usually man-made and their presence known in advance. Bridge pylons, piers, navigational aids, and lobster trap buoys are common examples. Since their presence is known in advance, how best to deal with them
can be worked out before fishing begins. Gordy Hill told
me of a strategy he and his fishing buddies use when
fishing for tarpon near bridge piers. As soon as the fish
is hooked, they apply heavy side pressure on the side
nearest the pier. If all works according to plan, the fish
fights against the pressure and in so doing moves away
from the pier and toward open water where they have
the advantage. A great example of indirect control is

getting the fish to go where you want it to without having to pull it there.

When it is not possible to get between the fish and the obstruction, try to position yourself so that the hook set is complementary to any moves you plan to make to keep the fish free of the obstruction. When fishing for sheepshead around pylons, for example, I present my fly on the side facing where I am positioned. In order to take the fly the fish must move away from the pylon. When it hits the fly I make a long sweeping strike, which is designed to carry the fish still farther from its lair. The greater the distance from the pylon, the more room I have to play the fish. This trick has also worked at times to keep snook from getting back in under the mangroves. I must caution that with any large fish the amount of time available in which to move it is very short. The move must be aborted the instant the fish fails to respond according to your plan.

In spite of the discussion above, which focuses on the handling of specific situations, the best general advice I can give concerning snags and obstructions is to fight all fish up close and personal. The greater the distance between you and the fish, the more likely the chance that something will go wrong. When, for example, a fish runs past a lobster trap buoy, you need to know on which side it passed. If you are not close enough to see what the fish did, you can only guess. Even if you were to guess correctly, you may not be able to control the fish since the ability to do so also diminishes with distance.

Having the opportunity to fish under varying conditions is, for me, like adding crushed red peppers on pizza—it adds a little extra zing and spices up my fishing. Whether the change is simply fishing from a boat to wading or just fishing new waters, staying alert to the demands of the new situation is important to success. Sometimes it is the challenge of catching new and different species that catches our eye. When this occurs it is a good idea to do some checking around to get some information about these fish and how they fight. A good boxer always knows his opponent.

FIVE

KNOW YOUR FISH

Knowing what to expect from a fish after it has been hooked is the fisherman's greatest advantage when fighting a fish. An investigation to identify the different escape responses characteristic of some of our more popular game fish reveals seven major responses: running, seeking shelter, leaping, diving, turning, rolling, and head shaking. Each escape response, singly or in combination, must be successfully countered by the angler if he is to prevail. To better prepare the fisherman for this task, each of the seven escape responses is discussed and an appropriate angler's response suggested. Table 5.1 identifies primary and secondary escape responses for popular game fish. Admittedly, getting this knowledge from reading a book is not as exciting as acquiring it firsthand, but any knowledge gained prior to the first battle with a new game fish is very worthwhile.

Table 5.1. Escape Responses of Common Game Fish

KEY: D = diving, HS = Head Shaking, L = Leaping, Ro = Rolling,
      Ru = Running, T = Turning, and SS = Seeking Shelter

Species	Escape Response Primary	Secondary	Comments
FRESHWATER SPECIES:			
Bass, Largemouth	D	SS, T	May leap at hook set then heads for cover.
Bass, Smallmouth	L,D	SS, T	Several leaps can be expected.
Pike, Northern	Ru, HS	Ro	Rolls when fatigued.
Muskellunge	R	T, D	Short run gives way to turning and diving.
Salmon, Atlantic	Ru	L, T	Spectacular leaps.
Salmon, Chinook	Ru	D, T	Strong runner with the tendency to stay deep.
Shad, American	Ru, L	T, HS	A strong persistent fighter.
Trout, Brook	T, Ru	Ro	Short runs and splashy turns and rolls.
Trout, Brown	Ru	D, T	Stays deep with persistent short runs.
Trout, Rainbow	Ru, L		Runs and leaps can be explosive.
SALTWATER SPECIES:			
African Pompano	D	T	Repeatedly dives then turns to surface before diving again.
Albacore	Ru		Distance runner with a strong heart.
Amberjack	D, Ru	T, SS	A powerful runner that seeks shelter in obstructions.
Barracuda	Ru	L, T	Lightning fast runs and leaps.
Bass, Striped	Ru, D	HS, SS	Runs well and a persistent head shaker.

| Species | Escape Responses | | Comments |
	Primary	Secondary	
SALTWATER SPECIES:			
Bluefish	Ru	HS, L	A poweful, hard fighting adversary.
Bonefish	Ru	T	Long-distance runner who turns to run again and again.
Cobia	D	SS, HS, T	A strong diver. Said to be able to match its own fight to correspond with the amount of pressure appplied by the angler and so pace itself for a long battle if necessary.
Dorado	Ru	HS, L, T	Fights broadside on the surface. Very acrobatic.
Fluke	D	T, HS	Hugs the bottom.
Giant Trevalle	Ru	D, SS	Seeks shelter in the coral.
Jack Crevalle	Ru	D	Similar to tuna.
Ladyfish	L, Ru	HS, T	Leaps repeatedly.
Mackerel, King	Ru	D, T	Long, powerful runs and dives.
Marlin	Ru	L	Very long powerful runs with spectacular leaps.
Mutton Snapper	Ru	SS	If running fails to free it, will seek cover.
Permit	Ru	D, T, SS	A versatile fighter willing to take you into the coral to escape. Stronger than Bonefish.
Redfish	Ru	HS, T	Runs are short but strong. Turns broadside and stubbornly resists.

(continued)

Table 5.1.   Escape Responses of Common Game Fish (*continued*)

KEY: D = diving, HS = Head Shaking, L = Leaping, Ro = Rolling, Ru = Running, T = Turning, and SS = Seeking Shelter

Species	Escape Response		Comments
	Primary	Secondary	
SALTWATER SPECIES:			
Roosterfish	Ru	HS, SS	Powerful runner and head shaker.
Sailfish	Ru, L	D	Long runs and high jumps. Often dives as a last resort.
Shark, Blue	Ro, T	HS	Hard to move. Notorious for twisting and turning.
Shark, Mako	Ru, L	D	Spectacular fighter with long runs and high jumps.
Skipjack	Ru	D	Small but a strong runner and diver.
Snook	SS	Ru, L	Heads for cover, right now!
Swordfish	Ru, L	D	Powerful deep runs punctuated with great leaps. Stronger than Marlin.
Tarpon	Ru, L, HS	T, D	Powerful head shaking leaps and strong runs. Will dive in deep water.
Tuna, Yellow Fin	Ru	D, T	Long runs and deep dives. Unmatched in staying power.
Wahoo	Ru	T	Long powerful runs. Rapid change of direction.
Weakfish	Ru	T, HS, Ro	Initial run followed by dogged head shaking, rolling and turning.
Yellow Tail, California	Ru, SS	T	Tremendous fighting ability and staying power.

Running

How fast a fish swims when fleeing danger has been exaggerated by some writers and underestimated by others. Assuming a conservative speed of fifteen miles per hour will serve to highlight the kinds of problems the fisherman faces whenever a fish decides to run. A fish moving at this speed will take out twenty-two feet of line every second. At that rate there is precious little time to clear any line that has been placed on the deck or in the water and see it safely through the guides without its becoming tangled. Line handling becomes the angler's first priority. As you will recall from the earlier discussion in chapter 4, this task is best handled by using the thumb and fingers of the line hand to form an "O" or tube around the line and then carefully funnel the line through the stripper guide. Once all the slack line has been taken up and the line is free to unspool directly off the reel, the angler can allow the fish to run against the drag. As the run continues, it is important to keep an eye on the amount of backing that remains on the reel. Running out of backing or being "spooled" is a real concern, for it carries with it not only the risk of losing the fish but the very real possibility that fly, leader, line, and backing will also be lost.

The best strategy to prevent being spooled is to have an adequate amount of backing in the first place. Freshwater fish are not known as long-distance runners and as such, with few exceptions, require little more than fifty yards of backing. Atlantic salmon and steelhead, especially when fished for in fast water, require at least 150 yards of backing. Two hundred yards of backing are usually sufficient for most saltwater game fish.

The amount of backing used on a given reel is determined by the size of the reel spool, the weight designation and design of the fly line, and the rated breaking strength or diameter of the backing itself. The use of thirty-pound dacron backing, for example, reduces reel capacity to 20 percent of that needed for twenty-pound dacron backing. In order to gain more room for backing, my personal preference is to use a reel one or two sizes larger than one designated for the line size I am using. I find the added break-off protection that the extra backing provides well worth the additional ounce or two of weight attributed to the use of a larger reel. Another option for increasing the amount of backing is to use backing made of gel-spun polyethylene that is less than half the diameter of traditional dacron. The use of gel-spun, however, has been slow to gain wide acceptance because it requires careful handling. Gel-spun tangles easily when not under tension, can cut flesh and loops made of doubled fly line with little effort when tightly drawn, and cost as much as 30 percent more than the dacron. On the other hand, in spite of being of smaller diameter, it is more abrasion resistant than dacron. Hence, it affords greater break-off protection when drawn across flotsam or fixed obstacles as well as longer life under normal circumstances. Regardless of how much or what kind of backing you may choose to use, it is recommended that you mark it with a permanent marker to indicate the point where only fifty yards remain. This mark will serve as a warning that you are about to run out of backing and allows time for any last-ditch efforts to stop the run.

It is quite natural that when talking about fish running that we assume the fish to be running away from the angler. Experience has taught us that this is what usually happens. However, it is not always the case. Fish that use running as their primary escape response are prone to make their first run away from the angler, and then reverse direction. As the fish draws closer, the angler faces increasing amounts of slack line. While this slack is not likely to cause the hook to lose its hold and fall out, a common but misguided belief, it does deny the angler the opportunity to keep pressure on the fish and to control it. A fish out of control is more likely to get tangled around an obstacle or snag. A personal experience serves to illustrate the point.

One day I followed a school of bluefish into a pod of lobster trap buoys thinking that if I hooked one, I would be able to keep it from getting tangled. So when I hooked a good fish and it headed straight for a trap, I was prepared, I thought. I lowered the rod tip to the side and applied as much pressure as I could afford. The fish turned and started toward me. However, before I knew it the fish was again in danger of getting tangled in a second buoy, but this time I was not in control. I had allowed my attention to be diverted and had missed the opportunity to recover the slack in the line, which resulted when the fish changed direction. I reeled in line as fast as I could, but not fast enough. My leader broke the instant the line hit the rope that secured the plastic jug marker.

Had I stayed focused on the fish, I would have realized that control was lost and steps could have been taken sooner to regain it. The angler should always respond to a slack line situation by reeling in all the slack and reestablishing control as quickly as possible. As mentioned in chapter 3, fishermen equipped with large arbor reels have a distinct advantage when it comes to recovering slack line compared to those who use more traditional reels with a slower rate of line retrieval. And, let me also remind you of the importance of staying as close as possible to the fish.

Seeking Shelter

Sometimes a fish runs in an attempt to reach shelter. Seeking shelter is in itself an escape strategy and as such needs attending to. Fish seeking shelter are played differently from those that just run. Running fish will tire in time, their energy having been used up in their many dashes to freedom. The angler's efforts are, therefore, directed toward maintaining the connection with the fish. When playing shelter-seeking fish, on the other hand, the angler's efforts are directed toward keeping the fish from reaching its shelter, be it rock pile, fallen tree, or kelp bed. Once within such obstacle-ridden surroundings, keeping the line and leader out of harm's way becomes a long shot. With the rod tip held low to the water, the angler applies maximum pressure to direct the fish away from where it wants to go. If the tactic fails, that is, the fish enters its shelter, the best option, as you will recall from chapter 1, is to give slack in order to reduce all tension on the line and then wait. Once the fright that sent the fish scurrying for shelter passes, you can expect the fish to leave the shelter. In the meantime, you can move closer to the fish. When the fight resumes, the fish, still tired from the first dash for cover and now closer, will be easier to control. That is, if not the first time, the second or the third.

Leaping

While a fish's sudden dash for cover can get your pulse rate up in a hurry, there is little that can capture a fisherman's attention so completely as when a fish jumps. This remarkable demonstration of speed and power can leave the best of us momentarily mesmerized and unable to function. But there is danger brewing and the angler must act quickly. Whenever a fish jumps there is the very real possibility that it will fall on top of the line on its way down. If the line is drawn tight when the fish hits it, the sudden shock could break it or tear the hook free. Whenever a fish jumps the angler must reduce line tension to lessen the severity of the shock. Usually this is accomplished by "bowing" to the fish.

Bowing is the term given to the act of creating slack in the line by leaning forward and extending the rod hand in a motion resembling a bow. Bowing is an effective way to create slack, but can create more slack than needed. Extra slack can be difficult to recover without creating shock when once again the line is tightened after the fish falls back into the water. Some experts recommend replacing the bow with a less dramatic lowering of the rod tip a few inches into the water. Which of these two responses is best? In general, it is the one you find most natural to do. However, when violent head shaking takes place out of the water, as is the case when tarpon take to the air, most experts would agree that the rod-tip-in-the-water technique is the one to use. The slight line tension that is maintained serves to help keep the hook in place under such adverse conditions.

Diving

The angler is at a disadvantage whenever a fish dives. The deeper the dive, the less control the angler has. When the fisherman is in a boat directly above the fish, the ability to apply side pressure is lost. The angler has few options: the first is to exert maximum pressure in the hope of getting the fish to abandon the dive. The angler should also explore every opportunity to change position in an effort to gain needed side leverage. Boat anglers have the option of moving away from the holding fish and then applying pressure from this new angle.

When a fish dives deep and holds close to the bottom, often referred to as sulking, the situation grows more serious. A sulking fish is a resting fish. The longer the situation is allowed to continue, the more time the fish has to recover its strength and the greater the risk of losing it. When the application of maximum pressure or changing position fails to get the fish moving, sending shock waves down the line by rapping a finger against the shaft of the rod will sometimes do the trick. This may sound a little far-fetched, but it does work often enough that you should keep it in mind.

Turning

Fish that turn quickly and change direction present the angler with several problems. The creation of slack line when a fish moves toward the angler and the loss of control that occurs has already been pointed out. In most cases, however, the change of direction is less dramatic and produces a loop or belly in the line. This belly acts much like a sea anchor to create additional pressure on the line. The situation is made worse when it occurs in moving water where the line is often pulled downstream by the current while the fish is moving upstream against the flow. In any case, failure to compensate for the increased pressure on the line can result in a break off. The angler needs to be on the lookout for any change of direction that might produce a belly and respond quickly by lifting line off the water in an effort to keep it following directly behind the fish. Sometimes if the fish happens to be very fast or the angler's response slow, the belly of line on the water becomes so large that any attempt to lift the line would break the tippet. Under these conditions reducing pressure to counter the increasing drag is essential. Once the run stops, the excess line in the belly can be safely retrieved.

The actual lifting of the line can take one of three forms. The first is to lift the line by raising the hand while keeping the rod tip nearly parallel to the water. This method avoids the additional, unwanted frictional drag whenever the rod tip is raised.

Raising the rod tip instead of the hand is the second way to lift line from the water. This method requires reducing line tension a little to compensate for the above-mentioned frictional drag.

The third method of lifting line off the water is really just a combination of the other two. The hand is raised up, not up and back, and the rod tip extended high into the air. I have heard this referred to as the "Orvis pose," a reference to the similarity it bares to the Orvis logo. The method itself is most useful when fishing for bonefish and permit on flats where mangrove shoots are a problem. Of the three methods, the combination raised hand and raised rod tip clears the most line off the water.

A different problem is created when a turning fish radically changes direction to present to the angler the side opposite the one on which it was originally hooked. While this reversed body position does not always mean that the hook's hold will be weaker, the possibility that it will be is ever present. As discussed in chapter 2, it is best to be less aggressive when applying pressure on the side opposite the one the fish was hooked on.

Rolling

Fish that roll in their struggle to free themselves often become tangled in the leader, wrapping it around their head, gills, or fins. The tangle may cause the angler to lose his ability to control the fish, or in some cases the tangle causes the line to be drawn over rough scales or sharp gill covers. The use of a shock tippet will help prevent leader damage due to abrasion, but does little to keep the leader from becoming tangled around the fish. The best way to prevent body tangles due to rolling is to keep the rod tip low to the water and positioned at a right angle to the fish. However, if rolling occurs some distance away from the angler, any efforts to prevent the fish from becoming tangled will most likely fail. The best way to free a tangle is to reduce line pressure and hope that the leader will free itself. Some anglers believe that by rapidly changing the position of the rod tip from high to low and from the left side to the right side will help clear the tangle. While this sometimes works, the results are unpredictable and at times counterproductive. One or two short periods of reduced tension on the line is usually all that is called for.

Head Shaking

Head shaking is not as common as running or leaping, but when it does occur it poses a real problem for the angler. Head shaking has the potential of creating shock severe enough to break the leader or dislodge the hook. This potential for damage is increased when the head shaking takes place out of the water, as is often encountered when tarpon take to the air. When the head shaking occurs underwater, the shock is somewhat dampened but still a concern. Head shaking needs to be countered by raising the rod tip to near vertical and backing off a little on line pressure. This maneuver doesn't change the force of the shock; rather, it enhances the ability of the leader, line, and rod to absorb it. Back off on line tension until the shaking stops and get ready for the fish's next move, which is soon to follow.

When head shaking takes place near the bottom, it may be an attempt to dislodge the hook. If allowed to continue it could weaken the tippet.

Gordy Hill, an experienced saltwater fisherman whom I introduced earlier, has witnessed this kind of head-shaking behavior among permit. Should you find yourself confronted with a similar situation, regardless of the fish species involved, it is better to move the fish off the bottom and risk the break off than to allow the head shaking to continue and risk damage to your terminal tackle.

Run, dive, leap—every effort to escape must be successfully negotiated by the angler. Knowing what to expect and then mentally or physically practicing appropriate responses is something that the inexperienced angler can do to sharpen his or her fish-fighting skills between trips. You might, for example, want to have a friend call out escape moves while you act out the appropriate response. The fish runs and you lower the rod tip. The fish heads for cover and you increase line tension and change rod position in an attempt to alter its course away from the cover. And, so it goes. Practice makes perfect.

SIX

HOOKING AND LANDING

Hooking and landing fish represent two important aspects of playing fish. One starts the fight, the other ends it.

Hooking

All hooking involves two basic operations. The first is to remove slack in the line. The second, to set the hook point and barb. If the hook is barbless, setting the hook involves burying the point as far as possible to the bend. The structure of the fish's jaw and the ease with which the hook can be set will largely determine which one of four hook setting techniques should be used. The four techniques are the lift-strike, strip-strike, modified strip-strike, and no-strike.

Lift-Strike

The lift-strike is the most common of the hooking techniques. It is a simple, almost instinctive act accomplished by raising the rod tip until the line is under tension and then accelerating the lift quickly to set the hook. Popular as it may be, the use of the lift-strike is seriously limited, being recommended for use only on fish with soft mouth parts such as trout, salmon, and bass. In order to understand where the limitations come from, think back to our earlier discussion on how the rod is used to play a fish. You will recall that the rod functions as a shock absorber to reduce or dampen shock to the line. The use of the rod, a shock absorber, to set the hook severely limits its ability to do the job. Those fishing in salt water will encounter many different species of fish with one characteristic in common—jaws of armor plate. For the toughest of these, the tarpon being an example, saltwater fishermen have devised the most powerful hooking technique in use today, the strip-strike.

Strip-Strike

When strip-striking, the rod tip is pointed directly at the fish so as to bypass its dampening effect. The line hand then strips in whatever line is necessary to remove all slack and then accelerates quickly and forcefully as when making a short haul to drive the hook home. This direct pull of the line with the line hand delivers the greatest force possible, but carries with it a need for caution. When the strike is made, the fish is likely to react violently by turning away or running. The angler must be prepared to release the line from the line hand to prevent it from becoming tangled around hand or fingers.

Another caution is in order when using the strip strike. Because of the force that can be generated with the haul and the lack of any shock absorption from the rod, it is very easy to strike too hard and break your tippet. This is exactly what happened to my friend George Simon on a fishing trip in Belize. After having his first ever tarpon throw the hook, George was bound and determined that it should not happen again. "You really got to set the hook, man," our guide Pedro said. Shortly afterward I watched as a tarpon turned to follow George's fly and slowly open its mouth to engulf it. He waited until the tarpon closed his mouth then struck hard with all his strength. At over six foot, George is no lightweight. The sharp crack of the breaking leader echoed across the flat. He had struck too hard and lost another chance at catching a tarpon, his second of the day.

I highly recommend you spend some time getting acquainted with the technique before you use it fishing. Try attaching your tippet to a tree or other stationary object and making a couple of strikes. If the tippet does not break, increase the force of your strike until it does. By experimenting in this trial-and-error fashion you will have a better sense of the force needed to give maximum hook penetration, which lies just short of breaking the line.

Modified Strip-Strike

A variation of the strip-strike, the modified strip-strike, involves a short sideward movement of the rod to remove any slack, then uses the line hand haul to set the hook. This technique reduces the risk of break off by positioning the rod to absorb some of the shock to the line caused by an overzealous hook set or violent reaction of the fish to the hook set. For this reason, the modified strip-strike is not as forceful as the strip-strike, but easier to master.

Not every strike leads to a successful hook set. If a fish takes short or for whatever reason fails to get hooked, there is a good possibility of a follow-up strike. That is, of course, if the fly has not been pulled completely out of the water by an overzealous hook set the first time. This is a common scenario when a freshwater fisherman uses the lift-strike and attempts to strike hard when fishing in salt water. The use of the no-strike technique solves this problem by having the fish itself set the hook.

No-Strike

When the fish takes the fly using the no-strike method the angler simply holds onto the line and allows it to tighten as the fish swims off. The advantage of this technique is apparent. As the fish moves away, the fly is drawn to the corner of the mouth for a more secure hook up without the risk of being pulled away by the hook set. The no-strike hook set is at the heart of the use of circle hooks, hooks designed to dig in only after passing over the edge of the jaw. The use of a circle hook makes it almost impossible to hook a fish so deeply as to cause injury to a fish destined to be released.

Having knowledge of the various hooking techniques can be for naught if the hooks that are used are not sharp. We are fortunate today to have access to chemically and electronically sharpened hooks from quality manufacturers such as Owner, Daiichi, Verivas, and others. Nevertheless, hooks do get dull and need sharpening from time to time. Hooks may be sharpened with a sharpening stone or fine-toothed file. The file is preferred because it is easier to achieve the triangular or diamond shape that serves as a cutting edge for ease of penetration. The point of the hook serves to anchor the hook and prevent it from sliding across bone or hard cartilage. A sharp hook has a point sharp enough to dig into the thumbnail with little pressure and a cutting edge to facilitate easy penetration. (See figure 6.1.)

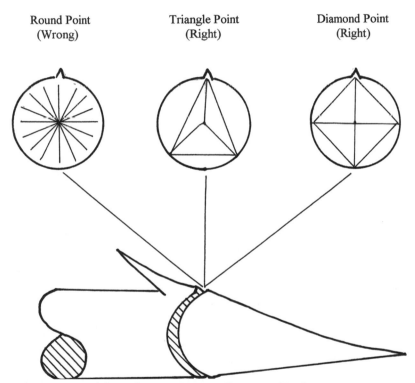

Round Point
(Wrong)

Triangle Point
(Right)

Diamond Point
(Right)

Figure 6.1.   Right and Wrong Way to Sharpen a Hook

When I first started sharpening my hooks, I found it helpful to practice using darkened hooks rather than bright ones. The removal of the black or bronze finish of these hooks during the sharpening process made it easier to see the results of my file strokes and to monitor the results. One thing to guard against is making the point too long. A long point is weak and can bend or break easily, ruining all you have tried to achieve by sharpening it. Keep the hook point short for greater strength.

Landing

As with other aspects of playing fish, having a plan is important when it comes to landing fish as well. Perhaps because more fish are lost at the time of landing than any other, it would be an even better idea to have two plans—a primary and a backup. Every experienced angler can recall a time when his net got hopelessly tangled, his gaff fell overboard, or some other glitch forced an immediate change of plans. This being the nature of the beast, it is important to know of the various methods of landing a fish and the conditions that govern their use. Netting is by far the most common method of landing a fish, but other methods include beaching, tailing, gaffing, use of the Boga Grip, and hand capture.

A landing net can be used in almost every situation but is indispensable when fishing from a boat, high bank, or rocky shore. Not only is netting the most common way to land a fish, it is also the most misunderstood method, that is, if technique has anything to do with it.

On the off chance that the Chinook salmon were on the move, I decided to explore a section of the Salmon River near Pineville, New York. After an hour or so of stop-and-go fishing, I hooked a salmon that was clearly larger than any I had ever caught before. There was no question in my mind that this was a fish I would really like to land. Since I had not brought a net, I began looking for a possible site to beach it when the time came. The willows crowded the rocky shore, dashing any hopes of a successful beaching. As I searched my mind for another alternative, I saw a boy of about eleven or twelve years of age walking along the wooded path. He was carrying a large net over his shoulder. "Hey, young fellow do you know how to use that net?" I asked. He said he didn't think so, but I recruited him anyway and positioned him about fifty feet below where I was standing. I told him to step into the water and away from the shore a little. I would bring the fish to him. I did as planned, but upon seeing the fish the boy made a lunge for it and off across the river it went in a terrible panic. I repositioned my young netter a little farther downstream and gave him instructions not to lunge at the fish. He was to leave the net in the water until I had brought the fish over it, then he was to lift the net. The boy waited patiently as I maneuvered the fish into position, but as it got closer to him he lost sight of it in the sun's glare on the water. Unsure of where the fish was, he lifted the net prematurely and again sent the fish to the opposite side of the river. Another failed attempt followed this one and by the time we were ready for the fourth we had moved downstream into a backwater and out of the main flow of the river. It was easier now for me to control the fish and direct the netting as well. The net was positioned in the water and as I brought the fish over it, I shouted, "Lift" and the boy lifted the net for the capture. I thanked him for his help as we stood admiring the fish. I will never forget the triumphant look on the boy's face as he walked toward me with net and fish held high. That was a great day for both of us.

When there are two people involved in netting a fish, the actions of fisherman and net handler need to be coordinated and complementary. The fisherman directs the action, giving the net handler instruction as to where to place the net. If you happen to be the net handler, follow directions carefully and when the fish is brought to the net, move quickly to force the head toward the bottom of the net bag. The most common and all too frequent mistake is to chase a fish with the net in the hope of capturing it with a quick swipe. Best to position the net in the water in advance of the fish's approach and leave it there until the fish is drawn to it. This serves to reduce the likelihood that the fish will be spooked in the process. If your attempt to net the fish fails, don't panic the fish further by trying for a second or third shot. You should reposition the net and stand still. Give the angler time to get the fish under control and bring it back for another try. Chasing a fish only serves to prolong the battle, increasing the chances of the fish getting free.

If you are the one fighting the fish, be sure to let the net handler know how and where to position the net. As the fish's head enters the net be sure that you release tension on the line. Forget to do this and the taut leader will make contact with the hoop of the net, preventing the fish from entering or breaking the tippet.

Netting is widely accepted as the most efficient and least harmful method of landing a fish. It was a shock, therefore, to learn that the use or possession of a net is prohibited when wade fishing some rivers in Alaska. Why, I don't know for sure, but I suspect for fear that it would facilitate poaching. In this situation, as in other situations where a net is not available, beaching is a very good way to land fish, especially the big ones. Beaching, however, is restricted to locations where there is a low-gradient beach. When attempting to beach a fish, the fish must first be brought as close as possible to the beaching area then turned to be slid head first onto the beach. Sounds easy, and it is, that is, when all goes as planned.

The key to successfully beaching a fish lies in using the forward movement of the fish as it fights to free itself to help drive it onto the beach. This situation only occurs when the fish's head is pointed directly at the beach. If the fish is able to turn, its forward motion is then redirected parallel to or away from it. Attempting to regain control by applying more pressure on the line as the fish moves away is to risk a break off. Best to abort the maneuver and let the fish go until it stops or slows sufficiently for you to regain the control necessary to once again bring the fish head first to the beach where another attempt at beaching can be made.

Unless a fish is to be killed, beaching is not usually used because the act of dragging it onto the beach is potentially harmful, risking damage to gills, eyes, and skin surfaces. The netless fisherman might want to consider tailing as a better alternative whenever the health of the fish or the lack of a convenient beaching site is an issue.

Tailing involves grasping a fish tightly by the wrist, that narrow section of the body just forward of the tail fin. Tailing may be done by hand or with a mechanical tailer. I am quite partial to tailing, especially for steelhead, salmon, and permit, for several reasons. First, I don't have to carry around a big oversized net, which I find to be a real nuisance when wade fishing. Second, I find the tail hold a secure one that helps to control the fish when removing the hook or positioning the fish for a quick photograph. Third, I find the act of tailing, especially by hand, to be the most exciting, up close, and personal way to land a fish, since it often requires that the fisherman be waist deep in the water and within inches of the swimming fish when the capture is made. Wearing a wool glove when tailing by hand greatly improves one's grip and is, therefore, highly recommended.

The mechanical tailer consists of a long flexible cable attached to a handle. When readied for use, the cable is doubled onto itself to form a loop similar to a lasso. The loop is passed over the tail of the fish and pulled tight around the wrist to make the capture. This method of landing a fish may not be as exciting as tailing by hand, but has several distinct advantages. The wire loop affords an extremely reliable hold and does so without scraping off a lot of protective mucus from the skin. In addition, the length of the handle serves to extend one's reach, making it easier to tail a fish from a boat or rocky shoreline.

Unlike tailing, gaffing is best restricted to professional guides and commercial fishermen. To do the job required of it, the point of the gaff must be keep very sharp. Used improperly, the gaff can maim both fish and fisherman.

When a fish is to be killed the gaff can be used in one of two ways: the most common is to reach across the back of the fish and draw the gaff into the flank. The alternative is to place the gaff under the water with the point up and strike upward as the fish passes over it. It is obvious that these gaffing techniques would not be used if the fish were going to be released. If this were the case, the gaff would be carefully positioned in the fish's mouth in such a way as to stick the gaff through the lower jaw. This sounds a little gruesome, but offers the best chance of survival when using a gaff. This same lip hold can be duplicated using a special tool called a Boga Grip.

The Boga Grip has two opposing pincher-like claws that come together on the fish's lower jaw to hold it securely. A scale built into the handle provides an accurate measure of the fish's weight as it is lifted from the water. The Boga Grip offers a safe, secure hold on any fish, but is especially useful when handling northern pike, barracuda, bluefish, and other toothy fish. Freshwater bass and saltwater species such as stripers, snook, and barramundi can be lip held by hand.

In this time of increased conservation awareness, many fish are never actually "landed" in the traditional sense. Rather, they are unhooked while still in the water and allowed to swim free without ever being handled. Dehooking tools such as the Ketchem Release Tool or surgical forceps can make the job easier, especially when barbless hooks are used. While I must confess to having some difficulty with using the Ketchem tool, John Mc-Cullough, an avid fisherman and friend, has experienced little difficulty. Here is how John describes his using the tool:

> When the fish is ready to be landed, I slide my line hand down the leader until I am about a foot away from the fish and then grab the line and hold it as I tuck the rod under my arm and ready the Ketchem Release tool in my rod hand. The tool is placed over the line below where I am holding and then allowed to slide down until it covers the fly. While still keeping tension on the line, I make a short jab with the tool to dislodge it then rotate my hand slightly as I remove the fly from the fish's mouth. The jab and the rotation are short and precise, requiring little movement of the hand.

Some fishermen are adept at grasping the fly in their fingers and, with a rotation of the hand, removing it cleanly. Again, let me mention that the use of barbless hooks facilitates the process. If you choose to unhook your fish while still in the water as described above, or by whatever method you choose, it is very important that you control the fish while unhooking it.

There is an increasing trend among today's anglers to reach down into the water and remove their fly without any contact with the fish whatsoever. While this has the appearance of being the most fish-user-friendly way to remove a hook, the practice can be harmful. As is often the case, the plan runs afoul when the fish panics, thrashes wildly, or bolts off. Caught off guard, the angler fails to release his hold on the fly and it is ripped out of the fish's mouth. How often have you encountered a fish with missing mouth parts? These fish are the victims of just this kind of release. Do not attempt to remove a fly until you have physical control of the fish and then do so carefully.

The best method to steady a fish for the unhooking is to use your net. Once in the net, lift the fish until it settles into the net bag. You do not need to take the fish completely out of the water to do this. With the fish supported as if resting in a hammock, the fly can safely be removed. I mention the use of a net because there are many who do not want to be troubled to use one, especially if the fish is small. Using the bare hands to capture a fish is neither recommended nor encouraged because of the damage it can cause the fish. Injury results from squeezing too hard as one tries to control the fish as it struggles to free itself. There also is the potential for harm in the angler's clumsy attempts at trying to grab the fish in the first place. Each unsuccessful attempt serves only to prolong the fight, which eventually leads to an increased level of exhaustion and the risk of death. At the very heart of every catch and release program is the requirement that the fish being returned are in the best condition possible. This having been said, let me direct your attention to the next chapter and what this means to you as a conservation-minded angler.

SEVEN

CONSERVATION/CATCH AND RELEASE

Nothing has had a greater impact on how we hook, play, land, and release our fish than the growing conservation consciousness and the practice of catch and release that it fosters. As a child growing up in the 1950s and in the twenty years that followed, I played each fish with only one purpose in mind—to add it to the others on my stringer. I would let the fish swallow the hook if it could and used only those with barbs. I wanted a secure hook up with little chance for escape. I played every fish to exhaustion, the safest and only way recommended by the experts of the day. If I didn't have a net, I would drag a fish up onto the beach as far as possible, concerned only that it might get away if unhooked too close to the water. Those where less-complicated times, killing your catch was accepted, it went with the territory.

But by the 1970s, the rate of killing was getting out of hand. The increasing population and the number of those who fished were growing steadily. Stricter catch limits proved of little value in halting the losses. The demands of fishermen for more fish was outstripping the supply. If allowed to continue unchecked, brood stocks would be endangered and survival of some species threatened. Strong conservation measures had to be taken. The reduced daily creel limits, slot limits, closed seasons, catch and release, and stocking programs in common use today are just a few of the ways fishery managers seek to maintain an adequate balance between supply and demand. The star of this lineup is catch and release.

Catch and release is the practice of releasing fish that have been brought to net rather than killing them. The practice may be required by law or self-imposed. Either way, its use and growth over the years is rooted in the desire to protect fish stocks. Lee Wulff, an ardent conservationist and proponent of catch and release, saw each released fish as one fisherman's gift to another. Little wonder that thousands of today's anglers practice it and encourage others to follow their lead. But all catch and release fishermen are not all the same. As you will see in the discussion that follows, they differ widely on such issues as the strength of commitment and the precautions they take to ensure that each released fish will survive.

Within the catch and release community there are individuals who always practice catch and release and, if they had their way, would require everyone else to do the same. They may even go so far as to release a fish they know is going to die just to avoid the shame or guilt they associate with killing a fish. On the opposite side of the ledger are those who only practice catch and release when required to do so by law. Seldom is any concern given to whether or not the fish will survive after the release. Should a fish die, they are apt to blame the waste on those who required that they re-

lease it in the first place. The vast majority of fishermen fall somewhere in between these two extremes.
There are those who release fish only after killing one
or two for dinner, regardless of a greater legal limit, or
release all fish except a once-in-a-lifetime trophy. The
extent to which we embrace the concept, however, is
only the tip of the iceberg. Once the decision to release
a fish is made, its chances of survival become the number focus of concern. How we play and handle fish to
be released differs from those destined for the table. It
is important to know these differences. My experience
on the Beaverkill one day will serve to illustrate the
point.

Guiding one day on the no-kill section of the
Beaverkill, I watched as a young man landed a nice
eighteen-inch brown trout. As soon as the fish was in
the net, he carried it several feet up the bank and de-
posited it upon a large rock in order to photograph it.
As he dug around inside his backpack for his camera,
the fish flopped off the rock. Our fisherman aban-
doned the search for the camera long enough to recover the fish and return it to the rock. Finally the
camera was located but not before the fish had once
more fallen from the rock. More time passed as the
fisherman repositioned the fish and took several pho-
tos. Pictures taken, he carefully returned the camera
to the backpack and then set about the task of releasing the fish as required. With all the tenderness he
could muster, the young man cradled the fish in his
hands and held it in the life-sustaining water. When at
last the fish began to move, he relaxed his hold and let
it slip away. Pleased with the catch and satisfied with
the release, he wiped his wet hands dry on his shirt
sleeves and turned to retrieve his rod, which he had
left nearby. He never saw the dying fish as it tumbled
in the current below him. Without the knowledge of

what he had just done, the young angler was destined
to repeat his mistake over and over. Just because a fish
swims away when released, does not mean that it will
not die later. Catch and release mortality occurs over
a span of hours or days, long after the angler has left
the water. The young man in the example above was
clearly a willing follower, but one not well informed
about fish physiology. Perhaps this is the place to
begin to introduce needed information with regard
to fish survival.

There is a generally held belief among research sci-
entists that a fish played to exhaustion will build up sufficient lactic acid so as to reduce the likelihood of its
survival. For example, studies conducted by biologists
R. A. Ferguson and B. L. Tufts at Queen's University in
Kingston, Ontario, Canada, reported a mortality rate of
12 percent for a group of rainbow trout exercised until
they no longer had the strength to resist capture. There
is on the other hand a common belief among fishermen
that fish should be played to exhaustion before attempting to land them. While tiring a fish can certainly
make it easier to control, to tire it until it turns belly up
is to be avoided for the reason cited above. If not to exhaustion, how long should a fish be played?

Some anglers use the formula of "one minute per
pound" for determining how long to play a fish. This
practice is widely accepted, especially among those who
fish for Atlantic salmon. It is precise and well grounded
in tradition, but not suitable when the plan is to release
the fish because it masks the importance of variables
other than time. The temperature of the water, for example, is a very important consideration for those who
fish for trout in the heat of summer.

As the temperature of water rises, it loses some of its
ability to hold oxygen. At the same time, this rise in temperature also warms the trout and increases its need for

more oxygen. Together, the decreasing availability of oxygen in the water, coupled with a rise in the trout's increased need for the same, seriously reduces the length of time it would take to completely exhaust a fish. Although a serious problem for trout, all fish are affected to some degree by changes in water temperature. Looking beyond the environmental factors, the manner in which a fish is played also affects how much time may be required to land it.

For many fishermen, fighting a fish is basically a physical tug-of-war, which, when done properly, must be completed in the shortest possible time. I am opposed to the use of time as the judge of good or bad practice. There is a very real possibility that scientific research may someday find that a fish brought to the net with the least amount of fright, as opposed to being in a state of sheer panic, will have a better chance of surviving after release, even if the process does take longer. The physical demands placed upon the body's metabolic systems are far more likely to fail under extreme short-term exertion than sustained low levels over time. Which would you find more taxing—running a four-minute mile or covering the same distance in twelve minutes?

There is not enough scientific data to say that one method of playing fish is clearly better than the other, that hard and fast is less traumatic than cool and slow. But when it comes to playing a fish to exhaustion, there is no doubt that it is harmful. Every precaution needs to be taken to prevent it from occurring. This includes being mindful of water temperature and not relying on time to determine when the fight should end. Land your fish at the first opportunity to do so, using a net to speed up the process.

While fishing for Atlantic salmon in New Brunswick, Canada, I hooked into a fish that weighed about eleven pounds. The fish was small in comparison to the tackle I was using so I took a very aggressive approach to playing it. I kept it in check, not allowing it to run or turn. Within a minute or two I was able to bring the fish to within two feet of the shore and hold it there. I looked to my guide to net the fish but he was not nearby. He had stepped back to get out of my way, planning to wait until the fish was exhausted before attempting to land it. By the time he realized that I had control of the fish and wanted him to net it, it broke free of my control and was later lost. This experience served to remind me that opportunities to land a fish may occur quite unexpectedly, and I need to be ready to take advantage of them whenever they do occur.

As I have been misguided in my early catch and release practices by my belief that a fish should be played to exhaustion before it is to be landed, so too have I been misguided by my belief that a fish that was held out of water suffered no more damage that a man did while holding his breath. That is, no harm would come to either as long as the duration of the activity was kept short. The study done at Queen's University and cited earlier reported damage to the gill's delicate lamellae when exposed to the air. The longer the exposure, the greater the extent of the damage and so too the likelihood that the damage would be permanent. When rainbow trout were exposed to the air for thirty seconds after being exercised to exhaustion, the mortality rate was 38 percent. This represents a 20 percent increase over those fish who were exercised to exhaustion but not exposed to the air. When the exposure to the air was increased to sixty seconds, the mortality rose to a whopping 72 percent. The full impact of these findings becomes apparent when one realizes that the decreased respiratory efficiency caused by damage to the gills is occurring at the same time that greater efficiency is required to overcome the rigors of the fight. Death follows the careless angler. I shudder every time I watch a fishing show and see the guide holding a fish out of the water while carrying on a long-winded conversation about how pretty the fish is, how fat it is, and on and on. I also shudder to think of the times in the past when I too have done the same.

Having a good understanding of fish physiology is one way to help decrease fish mortality. Knowing how to play a fish so as to increase its chances of survival is another way. There are few limits imposed on an angler doing battle with a fish he intends to keep. He is free to use all the strategies he knows and direct them to the single purpose of landing the fish by whatever means at his disposal. He may choose to fight the fish to total exhaustion then use a gaff to land it. However, once the decision to release a fish is made, the situation changes dramatically. The focus shifts from landing the fish to the survival of the fish after its release. Instead of fighting the fish to exhaustion, the angler must now watch carefully for any signs of it and quickly terminate the fight. A fish that is having difficultly keeping upright is nearing exhaustion and should be landed and released immediately or the leader cut to allow the fish to go free. Not only is the way we play a fish influenced by the decision to release it, but so too how best to remove the hook as well.

Recently I stumbled onto a catch and release article in which the author praised the practice of removing the fly without ever touching the fish. The directions to the angler were to grasp the fly with forceps and twist it free. As good as the idea may sound, it carries a risk of damage to the fish. Some consideration needs to be given to the extra energy spent as the fish fights to avoid the angler's attempts to get a firm hold on the fly. The antics that some fishermen go through to accomplish this task would be funny if it were not at the fish's expense. As mentioned in the chapter on hooking and landing, some concern need also be given to the possibility of damage to mouth parts, which

often accompanies the practice. Unless the fish is re-
strained in some fashion, a sudden and unexpected move
could leave the angler holding more than his fly. One out
of every three fish caught on the Beaverkill in the late season will bear the scars that tell the story of a fisherman's
poor technique or bad attitude. The use of barbless hooks
is often seen as the best way to reduce this kind of damage. However, while their use can certainly make removal
easier and less traumatic, it cannot take away the damage
caused by the movements of an unrestrained fish. How
best then to restrain a fish for unhooking?

The single best method of restraining a fish is to use
a net. The best nets for the job are those with flat bottom net bags made of a soft knotless nylon with small
mesh holes. The flat bottom bag allows the fish to lie flat
for easier hook access and removal. The soft mesh with
small holes helps keep fins and gills from becoming tangled. The net bag can also be used as a glove to help reduce injury caused by direct contact, should it be necessary to handle a fish. While handling fish in general is
to be avoided, it may become necessary to do so to facilitate a particularly difficult hook removal.

Catch and release is not the strict adherence to a
rigid set of laws. It is best seen as a conscientious effort
on the angler's part to look after the welfare of the fish
while at the same time enjoying the various aspects of
the sport that provide him pleasure. Consider, for example, what the fisherman who wants to take a picture of a
particular big fish might do.

When you photograph a fish you have killed, you
have all the time necessary to get your camera ready,
pose the fish, and take the picture, several shots if you
like. However, if you wish to photograph a fish you will
be releasing, the procedure needs to be carefully thought
out and planed in advance. Here is how I do it.

I carry my camera in a waterproof bag around my neck where it is readily available. As soon as I have the fish in the net, I have my fishing buddy or guide get the camera out. While unhooking the fish, I provide whatever instructions are needed for its operation. With the fish unhooked but still in the net and in the water, I position myself and explain the procedure to follow. First, he is to frame the picture and then on my command, I will raise the fish for the take. The command is given, the picture taken, and the fish is back in the water in three seconds or less. A close look at figure 7.1 reveals water still dripping from the fish as the picture was taken. When I am alone, I keep the fish underwater in the net until I have readied the camera. It helps to have a point-and-shoot camera for the job. The net is then raised to the surface and the picture taken. This usually produces a good picture, especially of the head, but the body is often hidden by the net frame. When a full body shot is desired, I move the fish to shallow water, being careful not to panic it, and take my picture before unhooking it. While this process does take some extra time, which might bring the fish closer to exhaustion, I feel it is better than exposing it to the air as it would be if the fish were stretched out on the beach. More damage is done through exposure to the air than exhaustion. Fortunately, only a few of my fish get photographed and fewer still are trout. Most fish are not as fragile as they.

Although our goal should always be to hook, play, and land our fish in such a manner as to make resuscitation unnecessary, the need to do so will arise from time to time. It is important, therefore, that every angler know the proper procedure.

When resuscitating a fish in moving water or from a moving boat, the fish is grasped lightly at the wrist of the tail with one hand and supported from underneath at a point just back of the pectoral fins with the other. The fish

Figure 7.1.   The command to raise the fish is given, the picture taken, and the fish returned to the water in three seconds. The author poses with a beautiful twenty-pound Bulkley River, British Columbia steelhead.

F. N. Franke Photo

is positioned to face head first into the flow and held in this manner until strong enough to break free and swim away. The water flowing directly into the fish's mouth is not required for normal respiration; rather, it serves as a stimulus and a supercharger, encouraging breathing and forcing a little extra water into the gills when it occurs.

When resuscitating a fish in still water, one should gently hold the fish in the water, and, if in a boat, move slowly forward. Many fishermen will use a back and forth motion, pushing then pulling. This practice is not recommended since pulling the fish backward is counterproductive, interfering with water moving over the gills rather than promoting it. If you feel it necessary to move the fish, do so by making elongated figure eights in the water. (See figure 7.2.) Resuscitation usually continues until the fish has recovered sufficiently to escape the angler's light hold. However, fast swimming fish such as albacore and tuna are best released by plunging them head first into the water.

The difference between catch and release fishermen and those who keep their catches is not as extreme as some would have us believe. Catch and release fishermen tend to look down their noses at anyone who would even think of keeping a fish. But the fact is that we all seek the same pleasure in our sport. We thrill at the landing of a bigger than average fish and share the same excitement when a fish goes airborne. The fact that a person chooses to keep the fish he catches does not make him less of a conservationist than the catch and release fisherman who shows little regard for survival of their catch after the release. Such a fisherman often kills more fish in a day than the angler who takes his limit and goes home. On my home water, the Beaverkill, it is possible to catch twenty or thirty fish on a good day. You can see how easily an uncaring fisherman could kill beyond his limit of five fish. What needs to be recognized, therefore, is that

Elongated Figure Eight
(Recommended)

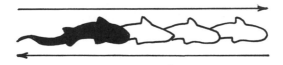

Push and Pull
(Not Recommended)

Figure 7.2.   Resuscitating a Fish in Still Water

all who fish have the potential to kill. This fact needs to be acknowledged and appropriate steps taken.

Since all fishermen will find themselves in a catch and release situation, either by choice or by law, I recommend using the catch and release techniques discussed in this chapter for all your fishing. This approach increases the likelihood that culled fish or those found not to be legal will live. This occurs in spite of the fact that one's initial intent may have been to keep it. Playing every fish as if it were to be released will make you a better fisherman. Doing your part to ensure that every fish you release lives will make you a better conservationist.

It has long been recognized that there are three stages in the life of a fisherman. The first is to catch as many fish as possible. The second is to catch only the biggest fish. The final stage is to catch only those that are considered the most difficult to catch. In recent times, however, a fourth stage has been added. This stage is one in which the fisherman seeks to give something back to his sport through active participation in organizations dedicated to conserving our natural aquatic resources. The Federation of Fly Fishers is the first such organization that comes to mind, but there are many others. The list below will get you started when the time comes that you feel the need to give something back for the sake of those who follow.

Atlantic Salmon Federation
P.O. Box 807
Calais, ME 04619-0807

Bass Anglers Sportsman Society (BASS)
P.O. Box 17900
Montgomery, AL 36141-0900
Phone: (334) 272 9530
E-mail: Bassmail@mindspring.com

CHAPTER SEVEN

Coastal Conservation Association
4801 Woodway, Suite 220W
Houston, TX 77056-1805
Phone: (713) 626 4234

Federation of Fly Fishers
P.O. Box 1595
Bozeman, MT 59771-1595
Phone: (406) 585 7592
E-mail: fffoffice@fedflyfishers.org

International Game Fish Association
300 Gulf Stream Way
Dania Beach, FL 33004
Phone: (954) 927 2628
E-mail: igfahq@aol.com

The Billfish Foundation
P.O. Box 8787
Fort Lauderdale, FL 33310-8787
Phone: (800) 438 8247
E-mail: TBF@billfish.org

Theodore Gordon Flyfishers
P.O. Box 2345
Grand Central Station
New York, NY 10163

Trout Unlimited
1500 Wilson Blvd., #310
Arlington, VA 22209-2404
Phone: (800) 834 2419
E-mail: trout@tu.org

AFTERWORD

As I travel around the country doing programs and holding clinics, I am frequently asked the question, "Do you ever lose a fish?" The answer is "Sure I do, but far fewer than I once did." I lose fish today for the reasons discussed in this book. Perhaps it was a poorly tied knot or my failure to anticipate the fish's movement and respond with the right amount of pressure or to give line. But what I do not do is say, "The fish was so big he broke me off." Not only do I not say it, I don't believe it. I can land any fish, IF I get everything right.

Being able to land a fish is not a game of chance, but one of skill. Accept that you are the one responsible for the outcome and you will add tenfold to your enjoyment of the sport. You, not Lady Luck, will be the one deserving of the credit for landing that biggest fish of your life. And, you never have to feel the helplessness inherent in the "fish broke my line" attitude. Time put into improving fish-fighting skills pays big dividends, to the fish as well as the fisherman.

Not all the fish we play will be big, and there can only be one "biggest fish of my life." However, how we play, land, and release the fish we do hook will have an impact on the quality of our fisheries in the future. Good fish-playing skills are important to you and to our sport. Enjoy!

BIBLIOGRAPHY

Apte, Stu. *Quest For Giant Tarpon*. (Video). Springfield, Ill.: Offshore Angler.

Borger, Gary A. *Presentation*. Wausau, Wisc.: Tomorrow River Press, 1995.

Brown, Dick. *Fly Fishing for Bonefish*. New York: Lyons Press, 1993.

Budworth, Geoffrey. *The Complete Book of Fishing Knots*. New York: Lyons Press, 1999.

Ferguson, R. A., and B. L. Tufts. Physiological effects of brief air exposure in exhaustively exercised rainbow trout (*Oncorhynshus mykiss*): implications for "catch and release" fisheries. *Canadian Journal of Fisheries and Aquatic Sciences* 49 (1992): 1157–1162.

Herzog, Bill. *Tying Strong Fishing Knots*. Portland, Ore.: Frank Amato Publications, 1995.

Janes, Edward C., ed. *Fishing with Lee Wulff*. New York: Alfred A. Knopf, 1972.

Kreh, Lefty. *Advanced Fly Fishing Techniques*. New York: Dell Publishing, 1994.

———. *Fly Fishing for Bonefish, Permit and Tarpon*. Birmingham, Al.: Odysseus Editions, 1992.

———. *Fly Fishing in Salt Water*. New York: Lyons and Burford, 1997.

Kumiski, John. *Saltwater Fly Fishing*. Point Pleasant, N.J.: Fisherman Library Corporation, 1994.

Linsenman, Bob, and Kelly Galloup. *Modern Streamers for Trophy Trout*. Woodstock, Vt.: Countryman Press, 1999.

Mitchell, Ed. *Fly Rodding the Coast*. Mechanicsburg, Pa.: Stackpole Books, 1995.

Phillips, Don. *The Technology of Fly Rods*. Portland, Ore.: Frank Amato Publications, 2000.

Quinn, Ralph F. *Ultra-lite Steelhead Fishing*. Merrillvile, In.: ICS Books, 1986.

Scharff, Robert. *Standard Handbook of Salt-water Fishing*. New York: Thomas Y. Crowell Company, 1966.

Sosin, Mark. *Practical Saltwater Fly Fishing*. New York: Lyons Press, 1989.

Sosin, Mark, and Lefty Kreh. *Practical Fishing Knots*. New York: Lyons Press, 1991.

Tabory, Lou. *Inshore Fly Fishing*. New York: Lyons and Burford, 1992.

Wilson, Geoff. *Geoff Wilson's Guide to Rigging, Braid, Dacron and Gelspun Lines*. Victoria: Australian Fishing Network, 1999.

Wulff, Lee. *The Atlantic Salmon*. Piscataway, N.J.: Winchester Press, 1983.

———. *Trout on a Fly*. New York: Lyons Press, 1986.

INDEX

ABOUT THE AUTHOR

For most of his 62 years Floyd has lived in two separate worlds. One devoted to fishing, the other to education and the opportunity it brings for personal growth. As time passed, these two worlds were brought ever closer together until today, when in retirement, they have merged. Fisherman/educator has become fly fishing instructor, guide, program presenter, travel host, and author.

"My greatest satisfaction in life," Floyd says, "is having the opportunity to share the sport I love with those who wish to learn more about it." The depths of his commitment to fishing and helping others learn is evident in his book.